Canadian Living

Healthy Family Meals

EXCLUSIVE DISTRIBUTOR FOR CANADA & USA
Simon & Schuster Canada
166 King Street East, Suite 300
Toronto ON M5A 1J3
Tel: 647-427-8882
Toll Free: 800-387-0446   **simonandschuster.ca**
Fax: 647-430-9446   **canadianliving.com/books**

Cataloguing data available from
Bibliothèque et Archives nationales du Québec.

Art director: Colin Elliott
Editor: Martin Zibauer
Copy editor: Ruth Hanley
Indexer: Lisa Fielding

07-17

Legal deposit: 2017
Bibliothèque et Archives nationales du Québec
Library and Archives Canada

Printed in Canada

Government of Quebec – Tax credit for book publishing –
Administered by SODEC.
sodec.gouv.qc.ca

This publisher gratefully acknowledges the support of the
Société de développement des enterprises culturelles du Québec.

 Canada Council   Conseil des arts
for the Arts   du Canada

We gratefully acknowledge the support of the
Canada Council for the Arts for its publishing program.

We acknowledge the financial support of our publishing activities
by the Government of Canada through the Canada Book Fund.

Canadian Living

Healthy Family Meals

BY THE CANADIAN LIVING TEST KITCHEN

JUNIPER
PUBLISHING
A Quebecor Media Corporation

SOUVLAKI-STYLE PORK TENDERLOIN
WITH MIXED VEGETABLES
p.34

Welcome to the
CANADIAN LIVING
TEST KITCHEN

Eating together as a family has many benefits. Research shows it leads to long-term healthier eating habits and may even boost kids' grades. Not to mention it just feels good to spend time together in the kitchen and at the table. Yet between sports practices, playdates and other scheduling conflicts, getting a meal on the table quickly isn't easy. That's where we come in. Bringing you deliciously healthy, trustworthy recipes is the top priority for us in the Canadian Living Test Kitchen. We are recipe developers and food writers, all from different backgrounds but equally dedicated to the art and science of creating great family-friendly recipes that are easy to make and successful every time. Plus, we have families too—we know exactly what you're going through!

WHAT DOES TESTED TILL PERFECT MEAN?

Every year, the food specialists in the Canadian Living Test Kitchen work together to produce approximately 500 Tested-Till-Perfect recipes. So what does Tested Till Perfect mean? It means we follow a rigorous process to ensure you'll get the same results in your kitchen as we do in ours.

HERE'S WHAT WE DO:

- In the Test Kitchen, we use the same everyday ingredients and equipment commonly found in kitchens across Canada.

- We start by researching ideas and brainstorming as a team.

- We write up the recipe and go straight into the kitchen to try it out.

- We taste, evaluate and tweak the recipe until we really love it.

- Once developed, each recipe gets handed off to other food editors for more testing and another tasting session.

- We meticulously test and retest each recipe as many times as it takes to make sure it turns out as perfectly in your kitchen as it does in ours.

- We carefully weigh and measure all ingredients, record the data and send the recipe for nutritional analysis.

- The recipe is then edited and rechecked to ensure all the information is correct and it's ready for you to cook.

TESTED
TILL
PERFECT
Canadian Living
TEST KITCHEN

CHICKEN AND KALE STEW ▶
WITH CHILI YOGURT
p.117

CONTENTS

SEARED SALMON WITH MANGO SALSA &
BUTTERY COUSCOUS
p.70

Healthy meals, happy families

ROSIE SCHWARTZ, RD

TEACHING OUR KIDS A HEALTHY APPROACH TO FOOD AND NUTRITION TAKES TIME, PATIENCE AND LOVE.

It's worth the effort, though—good eating habits can last a lifetime and provide lifelong health benefits. As parents and caregivers, we're role models in everything we do. Kids learn from what we put on the family dinner table and how we approach food. If you want your children to eat well and have a positive attitude to food, then so must you. Luckily, it's not difficult to lead by example.

A good way to show youngsters what makes a healthy meal is to offer foods that rate high in nutrients from at least three out of the four food groups: vegetables and fruits, grain products, milk and alternatives, and meat and alternatives. Focus the family conversation on how nutrient-rich options provide fuel for growing, running, playing and thinking, rather than vilifying "bad" foods that are fattening or cavity-promoting. Kids will make their own food choices when they're out in the world. By teaching them that sweets and other indulgences don't take the place of healthy choices, but are okay to enjoy occasionally and in moderation, you will help them understand how to balance their eating—and why it's important.

Be enthusiastic—adult eaters who approach new foods with anticipation, rather than trepidation, often pass this attitude on to the children around them. When you're open to trying new foods, your kids will be too. As a role model for healthy eating, try not to skip meals regularly, and don't berate yourself or other family members about eating habits or weight.

Getting the whole family involved in menu planning and food preparation encourages kids to touch, smell and taste food. When kids help prepare food, they are more likely to eat their creations, and they will expect other family members to do so as well. Appropriate food-preparation tasks will depend on the child's age and skill level, but there is opportunity for everyone to participate—and feel good about it. For example, if you ask your three-year-old to help you dress the salad, and then rave about how yummy it is, chances are good that he or she will

try some. Older children can even prepare some dishes for the family meal all on their own. Learning how to cook helps kids gain confidence and independence and is a factor in good health later in life.

For a balanced meal, aim to fill roughly half of your plate with less starchy vegetables such as dark leafy greens or cauliflower, one quarter with a whole grain or starchy food such as quinoa, brown rice or sweet potatoes and the last quarter with protein.

Research shows that ultra-processed foods, the ones with long lists of unpronounceable ingredients and additives, are the main sources of excess sodium and sugar in children's diets. Some processed food options, however, can offer both convenience and nutrition. For example, cans of tomatoes, fish and pulses (such as chickpeas, lentils or kidney beans), along with frozen vegetables and frozen unsweetened fruit make useful pantry and freezer staples that can round out a healthy meal in a flash.

The way you cook also affects the health of a meal. While cooking methods such as steaming, grilling, baking and stir-frying are healthier than frying, don't shy away from using healthy oils, such as extra-virgin olive oil and canola oil, in moderation. They enhance both the taste of the food and your body's ability to absorb fat-soluble nutrients such as vitamin A and lycopene (the red pigment in tomatoes). Spices and herbs boost flavour and allow you to use less salt, and these tasty ingredients are chock full of phytonutrients—compounds that promote good health.

Nutritious snacks are great options for all youngsters, whether they have small or large appetites. For those who eat only small amounts at a time, snacks help them get the nutrients they need. And for those who can eat large portions, a planned snack can help to tame a hearty appetite at the next meal. Think of each meal or snack as an opportunity for healthy family eating—a time to fuel up and get nutrients while enjoying the pleasures of food and one another's company.

JERK CHICKEN ONE-PAN DINNER
p.116

Slow Cooker Beef Barbacoa

HANDS-ON TIME	TOTAL TIME	MAKES
25 MINUTES	8¾ HOURS	10 TO 12 SERVINGS

In slow cooker, stir together tomatoes, red pepper, onion, jalapeño peppers, tomato paste, garlic powder, oregano, coriander, cumin, 1 tsp of the salt and ¼ tsp of the pepper.

Rub beef all over with remaining salt and pepper. Place in slow cooker, turning to coat; cover and cook on low until beef is tender enough to shred, about 8 hours.

Using tongs, transfer beef to cutting board. Let stand for 15 minutes. Using 2 forks, shred into bite-size pieces, trimming excess fat.

While beef is resting, use slotted spoon to transfer peppers and onion to large bowl, letting cooking liquid drain back into slow cooker. Skim fat from surface of cooking liquid. Add beef, 1 cup of the cooking liquid and the lime juice to pepper mixture; toss to coat. *(Make-ahead: Cover and refrigerate for up to 2 days; reheat in large saucepan over medium-low heat, stirring occasionally, for 15 minutes.)*

NUTRITIONAL INFORMATION, PER EACH OF 12 SERVINGS: about 233 cal, 37 g pro, 12 g total fat (5 g sat. fat), 11 g carb (2 g dietary fibre, 6 g sugar), 97 mg chol, 453 mg sodium, 858 mg potassium. % RDI: 5% calcium, 37% iron, 5% vit A, 20% vit C, 8% folate.

1	can (796 mL) diced tomatoes
1	large sweet red pepper, sliced
1	large onion, sliced
¼ cup	chopped drained pickled jalapeño peppers
¼ cup	tomato paste
1 tbsp	garlic powder
2 tsp	dried oregano
2 tsp	ground coriander
1 tsp	ground cumin
1¼ tsp	salt
½ tsp	pepper
1.5 kg	boneless well-marbled beef cross rib pot roast
1 tbsp	lime juice

TIP FROM THE TEST KITCHEN

Serve Beef Barbacoa in fresh tortillas with your favourite taco fillings. Or serve it over rice with sour cream and fresh herbs.

Slow Cooker Beef & Tomato Ragù

HANDS-ON TIME	TOTAL TIME	MAKES
25 MINUTES	8½ HOURS	8 TO 10 SERVINGS

2 cups	bottled strained tomatoes (passata)
1	can (156 mL) tomato paste
2 tsp	balsamic vinegar
1 tsp	granulated sugar
1	onion, diced
1	carrot, diced
1	rib celery, diced
¼ cup	diced pancetta
10	sprigs fresh thyme
2	bay leaves
2 tsp	dried oregano
¼ tsp	each salt, pepper and hot pepper flakes
900 g	boneless beef pot roast (top or bottom blade, or cross rib), trimmed

In bowl, stir together strained tomatoes, tomato paste, vinegar and sugar; set aside. In slow cooker, combine onion, carrot, celery, pancetta, thyme, bay leaves, oregano, salt, pepper and hot pepper flakes. Place beef over top; pour tomato mixture over beef. Cover and cook on low until beef is tender, 8 to 10 hours.

Discard thyme sprigs and bay leaves. Transfer beef to cutting board; let cool slightly. Using 2 forks, shred into bite-size pieces; return to slow cooker, stirring to coat.

NUTRITIONAL INFORMATION, PER EACH OF 10 SERVINGS: about 181 cal, 20 g pro, 7 g total fat (3 g sat. fat), 8 g carb (1 g dietary fibre, 5 g sugar), 48 mg chol, 291 mg sodium, 594 mg potassium. % RDI: 2% calcium, 24% iron, 16% vit A, 10% vit C, 5% folate.

TIP FROM THE TEST KITCHEN
Serve ragù, the classic Italian meat sauce, over pasta with grated Parmesan cheese and fresh basil. Ragù stores and freezes well; refrigerate in an airtight container for up to 3 days or freeze for up to 1 month.

Salsa Meat Loaf

HANDS-ON TIME	TOTAL TIME	MAKES
20 MINUTES	80 MINUTES	8 SERVINGS

In large bowl, lightly whisk egg whites; stir in oats, onion, zucchini, carrot, garlic, Worcestershire sauce, salt, thyme and pepper. Mix in beef.

Place on greased rimmed baking sheet; form into 13-inch long by 2-inch high oval loaf. Bake in 350°F oven until browned, about 40 minutes. Spread salsa over top; bake until no longer pink inside and instant-read thermometer inserted in centre reads 160°F, about 20 minutes.

NUTRITIONAL INFORMATION, PER SERVING: about 206 cal, 22 g pro, 7 g total fat (3 g sat. fat), 12 g carb (2 g dietary fibre), 47 mg chol, 382 mg sodium. % RDI: 3% calcium, 19% iron, 25% vit A, 7% vit C, 7% folate.

4	egg whites
1 cup	large-flake rolled oats
1	onion, grated
1 cup	grated zucchini
¾ cup	grated carrot
4	cloves garlic, minced
1 tsp	Worcestershire sauce
¾ tsp	salt
½ tsp	each dried thyme and pepper
750 g	extra-lean ground beef
½ cup	salsa

TIP FROM THE TEST KITCHEN
Cooking meatloaf on a baking sheet, rather than in a loaf pan, allows fat to drain away for a more healthful meal.

Beef & Broccoli Brown Rice Bowl

HANDS-ON TIME 10 MINUTES	TOTAL TIME 25 MINUTES	MAKES 4 SERVINGS

1 cup	whole grain 20-minute brown rice (such as Uncle Ben's)
2 tsp	canola oil
340 g	beef flank marinating steak, thinly sliced across the grain
¼ tsp	each salt and pepper
1 tbsp	minced fresh ginger
3	cloves garlic, minced
6 cups	bite-size broccoli florets (about 250 g)
½ cup	sodium-reduced beef broth
1	carrot, thinly sliced diagonally
1 tbsp	oyster sauce

In saucepan, add rice and 2 cups water; bring to boil. Cover, reduce heat and simmer until no liquid remains, about 20 minutes. Fluff with fork; keep warm.

Meanwhile, in large nonstick skillet, heat 1 tsp of the oil over medium-high heat; cook steak and half each of the salt and pepper, stirring, until no longer pink, about 3 minutes. Transfer to plate.

Add remaining oil, the ginger and garlic to pan; cook, stirring, until fragrant, about 1 minute. Add broccoli; cook, stirring, until bright green, about 1 minute. Add broth; cover, reduce heat to medium and cook just until broccoli is tender, about 3 minutes.

Stir in carrot, oyster sauce and remaining salt and pepper; cook, stirring, until carrots are tender-crisp, about 2 minutes. Serve over rice.

NUTRITIONAL INFORMATION, PER SERVING: about 380 cal, 26 g pro, 11 g total fat (3 g sat. fat), 46 g carb (4 g dietary fibre, 2 g sugar), 40 mg chol, 443 mg sodium, 659 mg potassium. % RDI: 5% calcium, 19% iron, 49% vit A, 60% vit C, 16% folate.

TIP FROM THE TEST KITCHEN
Thin bite-size pieces of flank steak are easier for kids to eat than long strips. Cut flank steak in half lengthwise (with the grain) before thinly slicing it crosswise (against the grain).

Shepherd's Pie Soup

HANDS-ON TIME	TOTAL TIME	MAKES
30 MINUTES	30 MINUTES	4 TO 6 SERVINGS

In Dutch oven or large heavy-bottomed saucepan, heat oil over medium-high heat; sauté onion, garlic and thyme until onion is softened, about 2 minutes. Add beef, carrot, celery and potatoes; cook, stirring and breaking up beef with spoon, until beef is no longer pink, about 3 minutes.

Stir in tomato paste, mustard and Worcestershire sauce; cook until slightly thickened, about 2 minutes.

Add broth and pepper; bring to boil. Reduce heat, cover and simmer until potatoes are tender, about 6 minutes. Stir in peas; cook until heated through, about 1 minute.

NUTRITIONAL INFORMATION, PER EACH OF 6 SERVINGS: about 262 cal, 19 g pro, 12 g total fat (4 g sat. fat), 19 g carb (3 g dietary fibre, 4 g sugar), 45 mg chol, 484 mg sodium, 558 mg potassium. % RDI: 4% calcium, 17% iron, 32% vit A, 17% vit C, 13% folate.

2 tsp	olive oil
1	onion, chopped
2	cloves garlic, minced
2 tsp	chopped fresh thyme
450 g	lean ground beef
1	large carrot, diced
1	rib celery, diced
450 g	white potatoes (2 to 4), peeled and cut in ½-inch chunks
2 tbsp	tomato paste
1 tbsp	Dijon mustard
1 tbsp	Worcestershire sauce
1	pkg (900 mL) sodium-reduced beef broth
¼ tsp	pepper
1 cup	frozen peas

TIP FROM THE TEST KITCHEN

Freeze any leftover tomato paste from the can in 1 tbsp portions (in an ice cube tray) for later use.

Florentine Meatball Subs

HANDS-ON TIME 30 MINUTES	TOTAL TIME 30 MINUTES	MAKES 4 SERVINGS

half	pkg (300 g pkg) frozen spinach, thawed and squeezed dry
4	cloves garlic, sliced in half
1½ tsp	Italian herb seasoning
1 tsp	Dijon mustard
pinch	each salt and pepper
340 g	extra-lean ground beef
2 tsp	olive oil
1	large onion, thinly sliced
1 tsp	balsamic vinegar
1 cup	bottled strained tomatoes (passata)
4	hotdog buns

In food processor, pulse together spinach, garlic, Italian seasoning, mustard, salt and pepper until finely chopped. Add beef; pulse just until combined, about 3 times. Roll into 16 balls; arrange on parchment paper–lined rimmed baking sheet.

Bake in 400°F oven, turning once, until no longer pink inside and instant-read thermometer inserted in several reads 160°F, about 12 minutes.

Meanwhile, in nonstick skillet, heat oil over medium heat; cook onion, stirring occasionally, until soft and golden, about 15 minutes. Stir in vinegar. Scrape into bowl.

Add meatballs and strained tomatoes to pan; cook over medium heat, stirring, until heated through, about 2 minutes.

Halve buns lengthwise almost all the way through; arrange on baking sheet. Spoon onion mixture into buns; top each with 4 meatballs. Spoon tomato sauce over top. Bake in 400°F oven until buns are warm, about 2 minutes.

NUTRITIONAL INFORMATION, PER SERVING: about 365 cal, 25 g pro, 12 g total fat (4 g sat. fat), 41 g carb (7 g dietary fibre, 11 g sugar), 47 mg chol, 496 mg sodium, 702 mg potassium. % RDI: 12% calcium, 36% iron, 30% vit A, 8% vit C, 26% folate.

TIP FROM THE TEST KITCHEN

The liquid in the spinach can dilute the meatballs' flavour and make them soggy. Wrap thawed spinach in layers of cheesecloth or a cloth kitchen towel and squeeze to remove excess liquid.

Ginger Miso Steak Salad

HANDS-ON TIME	TOTAL TIME	MAKES
15 MINUTES	20 MINUTES	4 SERVINGS

Rub steak all over with salt and pepper. In cast-iron or heavy-bottomed skillet, heat vegetable oil and butter over medium-high heat; cook steak, turning once, until medium-rare, 8 to 10 minutes. Transfer to cutting board; let stand for 5 minutes. Thinly slice across the grain.

While steak is resting, in bowl, whisk together cilantro, vinegar, miso paste, ginger, olive oil, garlic, chili garlic sauce and 3 tbsp water.

In large bowl, toss together lettuce, yellow pepper, cucumber and half of the dressing. Divide lettuce mixture and steak among 4 plates; drizzle with remaining dressing.

NUTRITIONAL INFORMATION, PER SERVING: about 303 cal, 28 g pro, 17 g total fat (6 g sat. fat), 9 g carb (2 g dietary fibre, 3 g sugar), 50 mg chol, 561 mg sodium, 732 mg potassium. % RDI: 5% calcium, 26% iron, 31% vit A, 100% vit C, 35% folate.

450 g	beef flank marinating steak
¼ tsp	each salt and pepper
2 tsp	vegetable oil
2 tsp	butter
2 tbsp	chopped fresh cilantro
2 tbsp	unseasoned rice vinegar
2 tbsp	white miso paste
1 tbsp	grated fresh ginger
1 tbsp	olive oil
1	clove garlic, minced
½ tsp	chili garlic sauce
2	heads Boston lettuce, torn
1	sweet yellow or red pepper, thinly sliced
half	English cucumber, halved lengthwise and sliced crosswise

TIP FROM THE TEST KITCHEN

White miso has a milder, sweeter flavour than yellow or red miso. Try this dressing on salmon or grilled chicken.

Steak & Asparagus Stir-Fry

HANDS-ON TIME	TOTAL TIME	MAKES
25 MINUTES	25 MINUTES	4 SERVINGS

2 tbsp	oyster sauce
1 tsp	chili garlic sauce
¼ tsp	each salt and pepper
450 g	beef flank marinating steak, thinly sliced across the grain
4	cloves garlic, minced
1	egg yolk
2 tsp	cornstarch
1 tbsp	vegetable oil
1	onion, thinly sliced
100 g	shiitake mushrooms, stemmed and sliced
1	bunch asparagus (about 450 g), trimmed and cut in 1½-inch lengths
1	sweet red pepper, thinly sliced

In bowl, whisk together oyster sauce, chili garlic sauce, half each of the salt and pepper and ⅓ cup water. Set aside.

In separate bowl, toss together beef, garlic, egg yolk, cornstarch and remaining salt and pepper. In large nonstick skillet or wok, heat 1 tsp of the oil over medium-high heat; stir-fry half of the beef mixture until browned, about 3 minutes. Transfer to plate. Repeat with 1 tsp of the remaining oil and the remaining beef mixture.

In same pan, heat remaining oil over medium-high heat; stir-fry onion and mushrooms until onion is golden and mushrooms are softened, about 4 minutes.

Add asparagus, red pepper and 2 tbsp water; stir-fry until asparagus is tender-crisp, about 6 minutes. Return beef and any accumulated juices to pan. Stir in oyster sauce mixture; cook, stirring, until slightly thickened, about 1 minute.

NUTRITIONAL INFORMATION, PER SERVING: about 284 cal, 28 g pro, 14 g total fat (5 g sat. fat), 11 g carb (3 g dietary fibre, 3 g sugar), 101 mg chol, 476 mg sodium, 664 mg potassium. % RDI: 4% calcium, 22% iron, 17% vit A, 93% vit C, 20% folate.

TIP FROM THE TEST KITCHEN

Coating thinly sliced meat with egg yolk and cornstarch is called "velveting." It's a common stir-fry technique that helps keep beef and chicken tender.

Mexican-Style Flatbreads

HANDS-ON TIME	TOTAL TIME	MAKES
25 MINUTES	25 MINUTES	4 SERVINGS

In nonstick skillet, heat oil over medium heat; cook onion, stirring often, until softened, about 7 minutes. Add beef; cook, breaking up with spoon, until browned on the outside but not cooked through, about 2 minutes. Add garlic, chili powder, coriander, cumin and salt; cook, stirring, until beef is no longer pink, about 3 minutes.

Add corn, 2 tbsp of the sour cream and 2 tbsp water; cook, stirring, until corn is heated through and mixture is slightly saucy, about 2 minutes. Stir in half of the cilantro.

Spoon beef mixture over pitas; top with tomato, lettuce and remaining sour cream and cilantro.

NUTRITIONAL INFORMATION, PER SERVING: about 375 cal, 24 g pro, 18 g total fat (6 g sat. fat), 32 g carb (3 g dietary fibre, 4 g sugar), 55 mg chol, 413 mg sodium, 522 mg potassium. % RDI: 6% calcium, 26% iron, 9% vit A, 12% vit C, 15% folate.

2 tsp	olive oil
1	onion, sliced
340 g	lean ground beef
3	cloves garlic, minced
2 tsp	chili powder
½ tsp	each ground coriander and ground cumin
¼ tsp	salt
¾ cup	frozen corn kernels
3 tbsp	sour cream
½ cup	chopped fresh cilantro
2	whole wheat pita pockets (6 inches), split horizontally in two rounds and toasted
1	Roma tomato, seeded and chopped
1 cup	shredded iceberg lettuce

TIP FROM THE TEST KITCHEN
To split pitas quickly and easily, snip the edge with kitchen scissors.

Mini Shepherd's Pies
WITH ROASTED CARROT & TOMATO SALAD

HANDS-ON TIME	TOTAL TIME	MAKES
35 MINUTES	1¼ HOURS	4 SERVINGS

SHEPHERD'S PIES

1	small onion, quartered
half	pkg (227 g pkg) cremini mushrooms
2	cloves garlic
450 g	extra-lean ground beef
1 tsp	olive oil
½ tsp	dried rosemary
1 tbsp	all-purpose flour
¼ cup	each frozen corn and frozen peas
1 tsp	Worcestershire sauce
½ tsp	each salt and pepper
675 g	yellow-fleshed potatoes, peeled and cut in 1-inch chunks
2 tbsp	butter
2	green onions, sliced

CARROT AND TOMATO SALAD

3	large carrots
1 cup	grape tomatoes or cherry tomatoes, halved
2 tbsp	olive oil
1 tbsp	balsamic vinegar
pinch	each salt and pepper
4 cups	lightly packed baby salad greens

SHEPHERD'S PIES In food processor, pulse together onion, mushrooms and garlic until finely chopped. Set aside.

In large nonstick skillet, cook beef over medium-high heat, breaking up with spoon, until no longer pink, about 8 minutes. Scrape into bowl. In same pan, heat oil over medium-high heat; sauté onion mixture and rosemary until no liquid remains, about 4 minutes. Sprinkle with flour; cook, stirring often, for 2 minutes. Stir in corn, peas, Worcestershire sauce, half each of the salt and pepper and 1 cup water. Add beef and any juices; bring to boil. Reduce heat and simmer, stirring, until thickened, about 2 minutes. Divide among four 1½-cup ramekins.

Meanwhile, in large saucepan of boiling lightly salted water, cook potatoes until tender, about 12 minutes. Reserving ½ cup of the cooking liquid, drain. Return potatoes to saucepan; mash with half of the butter, the remaining salt and pepper and reserved cooking liquid, as needed, until smooth. Stir in green onions. Spoon over beef mixture, spreading to rims of ramekins. *(Make-ahead: Cover and refrigerate for up to 2 days; add 20 minutes to bake time.)* Dot tops with remaining butter. Bake on rimmed baking sheet in 400°F oven until tops are golden, about 30 minutes.

CARROT AND TOMATO SALAD Meanwhile, peel carrots; cut into 1½-inch lengths and halve lengthwise. Toss with tomatoes and 2 tsp of the oil; spread on parchment paper–lined baking sheet. Bake on bottom rack of 400°F oven, turning once, until carrots are tender, about 30 minutes. Let cool on sheet for 5 minutes. In large bowl, whisk together vinegar, salt, pepper and remaining oil. Add carrot mixture and salad greens; toss to coat. Serve with shepherd's pies.

NUTRITIONAL INFORMATION, PER SERVING: about 503 cal, 30 g pro, 23 g total fat (8 g sat. fat), 46 g carb (7 g dietary fibre, 8 g sugar), 77 mg chol, 780 mg sodium, 1,468 mg potassium. % RDI: 10% calcium, 32% iron, 180% vit A, 50% vit C, 51% folate.

Pork & Thai Pepper Bowls

HANDS-ON TIME	TOTAL TIME	MAKES
25 MINUTES	25 MINUTES	4 SERVINGS

Mince half of the Thai pepper; thinly slice remaining half. Set aside.

In large nonstick skillet, cook pork and salt over medium-high heat, breaking up pork with spoon, until no longer pink, about 8 minutes. Scrape into bowl. Set aside.

In same pan, heat half of the oil over medium heat; cook green beans, garlic, ginger and minced Thai pepper, stirring occasionally, until green beans are tender-crisp, about 5 minutes. Add pork, vinegar, fish sauce, brown sugar and 2 tbsp water; cook, stirring, until heated through, about 2 minutes. Divide among 4 serving bowls; keep warm. Wipe pan clean.

In same pan, heat remaining oil over medium heat; cook eggs until whites are set yet yolks are still runny, about 3 minutes.

Arrange 1 egg over each pork bowl. Sprinkle with cilantro and green onions (if using) and remaining Thai pepper.

NUTRITIONAL INFORMATION, PER SERVING: about 414 cal, 29 g pro, 30 g total fat (9 g sat. fat), 7 g carb (1 g dietary fibre, 2 g sugar), 266 mg chol, 206 mg sodium, 511 mg potassium. % RDI: 6% calcium, 16% iron, 14% vit A, 12% vit C, 24% folate.

1	Thai bird's-eye pepper
450 g	lean ground pork
pinch	salt
2 tbsp	vegetable oil
2 cups	green beans, cut in ½-inch pieces
3	cloves garlic, minced
4 tsp	grated fresh ginger
1 tbsp	unseasoned rice vinegar
1 tsp	fish sauce
½ tsp	packed brown sugar
4	eggs
½ cup	chopped fresh cilantro (optional)
2	green onions, sliced (optional)

TIP FROM THE TEST KITCHEN

Thai bird's-eye peppers are small and fiery hot. If you prefer a mild dish, reduce the amount of Thai pepper or use a pepper with less heat, such as jalapeño.

Crispy Japanese-Style Pork
WITH SESAME SLAW

HANDS-ON TIME 25 MINUTES	TOTAL TIME 30 MINUTES	MAKES 4 SERVINGS

RICE

1 cup	long-grain rice, rinsed

CRISPY PORK

¾ cup	panko bread crumbs
4 tsp	vegetable oil
1	green onion, minced
4	boneless pork loin chops (about 450 g total)
¼ tsp	each salt and pepper
¼ cup	all-purpose flour
1	egg, lightly beaten

SESAME SLAW

1 tsp	white miso paste
1 tsp	warm water
3 tbsp	vegetable oil
1 tbsp	seasoned rice vinegar
1 tsp	minced peeled fresh ginger
1 tsp	liquid honey
1 tsp	sesame oil
4 cups	coleslaw mix or shredded cabbage
¼ cup	thinly sliced onion
1½ tsp	sesame seeds, toasted

RICE In saucepan, cook rice according to package instructions. Fluff with fork. Keep warm.

CRISPY PORK While rice is cooking, in small skillet, mix bread crumbs with oil; cook over medium-high heat, stirring, until golden, 4 to 5 minutes. Transfer to shallow bowl; stir in green onion. Set aside.

Between plastic wrap or waxed paper, use meat mallet or bottom of heavy pan to flatten pork to ½-inch thickness. Sprinkle pork all over with salt and pepper. Dredge in flour, shaking off excess. Dip in egg, letting excess drip off. Dredge in bread crumb mixture, pressing to adhere.

Arrange pork on lightly greased rimmed baking sheet. Bake in 425°F oven, turning once, until juices run clear when pork is pierced and just a hint of pink remains inside, about 10 minutes. Broil until crisp, 1 to 2 minutes. Transfer to rack set over rimmed baking sheet; let stand for 2 minutes. Cut crosswise into strips.

SESAME SLAW While pork is baking, in large bowl, whisk together miso paste and warm water until miso paste is dissolved; whisk in vegetable oil, vinegar, ginger, honey and sesame oil. Add coleslaw mix, onion and sesame seeds; toss to coat. Serve with pork and rice.

NUTRITIONAL INFORMATION, PER SERVING: about 593 cal, 32 g pro, 28 g total fat (6 g sat. fat), 53 g carb (3 g dietary fibre, 6 g sugar), 96 mg chol, 423 mg sodium, 474 mg potassium. % RDI: 5% calcium, 12% iron, 12% vit A, 30% vit C, 20% folate.

TIP FROM THE TEST KITCHEN
Sesame seeds contain oil that can go rancid; don't buy them in large quantities. To help keep their flavour fresh, store in the freezer until you're ready to use them.

Orange-Glazed Pork Chops
WITH HAZELNUT GREEN BEANS

HANDS-ON TIME	TOTAL TIME	MAKES
20 MINUTES	20 MINUTES	4 SERVINGS

GLAZED PORK CHOPS Sprinkle pork with salt and pepper. In large nonstick skillet, heat half of the oil over medium heat; cook pork until juices run clear when pork is pierced and just a hint of pink remains inside, 8 to 12 minutes. Transfer to plate. Drain any fat from pan.

In same pan, heat remaining oil over medium heat; cook garlic and ginger until fragrant, about 2 minutes. Stir in broth and orange juice; bring to boil. Boil, stirring often, until thick enough to coat back of spoon, about 6 minutes.

Return pork and any juices to pan; cook, turning once, until glazed, about 2 minutes.

GREEN BEANS Meanwhile, in large saucepan of boiling salted water, cook green beans until tender-crisp, 2 to 3 minutes; drain. In bowl, combine green beans, olive oil, lemon juice, garlic, salt and pepper; top with hazelnuts. Serve with pork.

NUTRITIONAL INFORMATION, PER SERVING: about 358 cal, 31 g pro, 21 g total fat (4 g sat. fat), 14 g carb (3 g dietary fibre, 5 g sugar), 77 mg chol, 430 mg sodium, 628 mg potassium. % RDI: 8% calcium, 16% iron, 7% vit A, 38% vit C, 25% folate.

GLAZED PORK CHOPS

4	bone-in pork chops (about 790 g total)
pinch	each salt and pepper
2 tsp	vegetable oil
2	cloves garlic, minced
2 tsp	grated fresh ginger
1 cup	sodium-reduced chicken broth
½ cup	orange juice

GREEN BEANS

450 g	green beans, trimmed
1 tbsp	extra-virgin olive oil
2 tsp	lemon juice
1	clove garlic, minced
pinch	each salt and pepper
⅓ cup	chopped roasted hazelnuts

TIP FROM THE TEST KITCHEN
Try this dish with chicken breasts or thighs, cooking until the juices run clear when the chicken is pierced.

Lemongrass Pork Chops & Grilled Corn
WITH GINGER BUTTER

HANDS-ON TIME	TOTAL TIME	MAKES
30 MINUTES	6½ HOURS	4 SERVINGS

2	cloves garlic, pressed or grated
2 tbsp	grated lemongrass
2 tbsp	packed brown sugar
1 tbsp	fish sauce
2 tsp	sesame oil
1 tsp	vegetable oil
4	boneless pork loin chops (about 450 g total)
2 tbsp	butter, melted
1 tbsp	grated fresh ginger
4	corn cobs, husked
1 tsp	lime juice
pinch	salt

In large bowl, whisk together garlic, lemongrass, brown sugar, fish sauce, sesame oil and vegetable oil. Add pork chops; toss to coat. Cover and refrigerate for 6 hours, turning once. *(Make-ahead: Refrigerate for up to 12 hours.)*

In small bowl, combine butter and ginger. Place corn on greased grill over medium-high heat; close lid and grill, turning occasionally, until beginning to soften, about 7 minutes. Brush with butter mixture; continue to grill, brushing occasionally with butter mixture, until grill-marked and tender, 12 to 15 minutes. Drizzle with lime juice; sprinkle with salt.

Meanwhile, place pork on greased grill over medium-high heat; close lid and grill, turning once, until juices run clear when pork is pierced and just a hint of pink remains inside, about 8 minutes. Serve with corn.

NUTRITIONAL INFORMATION, PER SERVING: about 337 cal, 29 g pro, 11 g total fat (5 g sat. fat), 34 g carb (3 g dietary fibre, 6 g sugar), 67 mg chol, 231 mg sodium, 652 mg potassium. % RDI: 1% calcium, 11% iron, 8% vit A, 15% vit C, 28% folate.

TIP FROM THE TEST KITCHEN
To grate lemongrass, start by cutting off the woody ends and peeling away outer layers, then grate using a rasp.

Slow Cooker Pork Roast
WITH TOMATO AND FENNEL

HANDS-ON TIME	TOTAL TIME	MAKES
30 MINUTES	8¾ HOURS	8 SERVINGS

Stir together garlic, oil, thyme, fennel seeds, sage, salt and pepper. Rub half of the mixture over pork; set aside.

In slow cooker, combine celery, fennel, onion, olives, bay leaves, lemon zest and remaining garlic mixture; stir in strained tomatoes. Arrange pork over top. Cover and cook on low until pork is tender, about 8 hours.

Transfer pork to plate; tent with foil. Skim fat from tomato mixture. Discard bay leaves and lemon zest.

Remove 1 cup of the tomato mixture; whisk with flour. Whisk back into slow cooker. Cover and cook on high until slightly thickened, about 20 minutes. Stir in parsley. Slice pork; serve with tomato-fennel sauce.

NUTRITIONAL INFORMATION, PER SERVING: about 406 cal, 44 g pro, 20 g total fat (7 g sat. fat), 9 g carb (2 g dietary fibre, 4 g sugar), 142 mg chol, 477 mg sodium, 967 mg potassium. % RDI: 5% calcium, 31% iron, 3% vit A, 15% vit C, 13% folate.

6	cloves garlic, minced
2 tsp	olive oil
1½ tsp	dried thyme
1 tsp	fennel seeds, crushed
½ tsp	crumbled dried sage
½ tsp	each salt and pepper
1.8 kg	boneless pork shoulder blade roast, trimmed
2	ribs celery, sliced
1	bulb fennel, quartered, cored and thinly sliced crosswise
1	onion, quartered and thinly sliced crosswise
¼ cup	Kalamata olives, pitted and halved
2	bay leaves
1	strip lemon zest
1½ cups	bottled strained tomatoes (passata)
3 tbsp	all-purpose flour
¼ cup	chopped fresh parsley

TIP FROM THE TEST KITCHEN
Serve this dish over cooked pasta. You can use any leftover pork in Roast Pork Tacos With Apple Cucumber Salsa, page 30.

Roast Pork Tacos
WITH APPLE CUCUMBER SALSA

HANDS-ON TIME 25 MINUTES	TOTAL TIME 25 MINUTES	MAKES 4 SERVINGS

APPLE CUCUMBER SALSA

1	apple, cored and diced (about 1⅓ cups)
¾ cup	diced English cucumber
1	green onion, thinly sliced
half	jalapeño pepper, seeded and finely diced
¼ cup	chopped fresh cilantro
2 tbsp	lime juice
1 tbsp	vegetable oil
pinch	salt

TACOS

1 tbsp	vegetable oil
1	onion, thinly sliced
2	cloves garlic, thinly sliced
1 tsp	ancho chili powder or chipotle chili powder
1 tsp	each ground cumin and ground coriander
¼ tsp	each salt and pepper
2 cups	thinly sliced cooked roast pork, chopped or shredded
8	soft corn tortillas (6 inches), heated

APPLE CUCUMBER SALSA In bowl, stir together apple, cucumber, green onion, jalapeño pepper, cilantro, lime juice, oil and salt. Set aside.

TACOS In large nonstick skillet, heat oil over medium heat; cook onion and garlic, stirring occasionally, until softened, about 4 minutes. Add chili powder, cumin, coriander, salt and pepper; cook, stirring, for 2 minutes.

Stir in pork and ½ cup water; bring to boil. Reduce heat and simmer, stirring, until heated through, 3 to 5 minutes. Serve in tortillas; top with salsa.

NUTRITIONAL INFORMATION, PER SERVING: about 412 cal, 24 g pro, 17 g total fat (3 g sat. fat), 39 g carb (4 g dietary fibre, 6 g sugar), 51 mg chol, 486 mg sodium, 416 mg potassium. % RDI: 7% calcium, 17% iron, 4% vit A, 13% vit C, 6% folate.

TIP FROM THE TEST KITCHEN
Heat tortillas gently in a dry skillet and wrap them in a clean tea towel to keep warm.

Roast Pork Tenderloin
WITH ASPARAGUS & WARM CITRUS SAUCE

HANDS-ON TIME	TOTAL TIME	MAKES
15 MINUTES	30 MINUTES	4 SERVINGS

Stir together almonds, parsley and lemon juice; set aside.

Sprinkle pork with half each of the salt and pepper. In nonstick skillet, heat half of the oil over medium-high heat; brown pork all over, about 6 minutes. Transfer pork and asparagus to foil-lined rimmed baking sheet. Sprinkle asparagus with remaining salt and pepper. Bake in 400°F oven until instant-read thermometer inserted into thickest part of pork reads 160°F or juices run clear when pork is pierced and just a hint of pink remains inside, about 15 minutes. Transfer asparagus to bowl; keep warm. Transfer pork to cutting board; tent with foil. Let stand for 5 minutes before slicing.

Add remaining oil to skillet; heat over medium heat. Cook ginger and garlic, stirring, for 2 minutes. Stir in broth and orange juice; bring to boil. Stirring often, reduce sauce to ½ cup, 5 to 7 minutes. Stir in mustard and orange zest.

Meanwhile, cook rice according to package instructions; serve with pork, asparagus and sauce. Sprinkle with almond mixture.

NUTRITIONAL INFORMATION, PER SERVING: about 379 cal, 32 g pro, 11 g total fat (2 g sat. fat), 41 g carb (5 g dietary fibre, 5 g sugar), 54 mg chol, 344 mg sodium, 854 mg potassium. % RDI: 8% calcium, 23% iron, 18% vit A, 45% vit C, 117% folate.

¼ cup	natural (skin-on) almonds, chopped
2 tbsp	chopped fresh parsley
2 tsp	lemon juice
400 g	pork tenderloin, trimmed if necessary
¼ tsp	each salt and pepper
1 tbsp	olive oil
2	bunches (each 450 g) asparagus, trimmed
1 tbsp	grated fresh ginger
2	cloves garlic, minced
¾ cup	sodium-reduced chicken broth
½ tsp	grated orange zest
½ cup	orange juice
1 tsp	Dijon mustard
¾ cup	basmati rice

TIP FROM THE TEST KITCHEN
When you buy a pork tenderloin, it may still have shiny connective tissue, or "silverskin," on the meat's surface. Unlike fat, silverskin doesn't melt or soften, so you should trim it with a sharp knife.

Souvlaki-Style Pork Tenderloin
WITH MIXED VEGETABLES

📷 p.4

HANDS-ON TIME	TOTAL TIME	MAKES
25 MINUTES	30 MINUTES	4 SERVINGS

PORK TENDERLOIN

450 g	pork tenderloin
2 tsp	dried oregano
½ tsp	pepper
¼ tsp	salt
2 tsp	olive oil
450 g	sweet potatoes, peeled and cut in ½-inch chunks
1	red onion, cut in ¾-inch chunks
2	cloves garlic, minced
½ cup	sodium-reduced chicken broth
2	zucchini, cut in ¾-inch chunks
1	sweet red pepper, cut in ¾-inch chunks
4 tsp	lemon juice

GARLIC YOGURT SAUCE

⅓ cup	0% plain Greek yogurt
1	small clove garlic, minced

PORK TENDERLOIN Sprinkle pork with ½ tsp of the oregano and half each of the pepper and salt.

In large nonstick skillet, heat half of the oil over medium-high heat; brown pork all over, about 5 minutes. Transfer to foil-lined rimmed baking sheet; bake in 425°F oven until instant-read thermometer inserted into thickest part of pork reads 160°F or juices run clear when pork is pierced and just a hint of pink remains inside, about 12 minutes. Transfer to cutting board; let stand for 3 minutes before slicing.

Meanwhile, in same pan, heat remaining oil over medium heat; cook sweet potatoes, stirring, until lightly browned, about 3 minutes. Stir in onion, garlic and remaining oregano. Cook, stirring often, until onions are slightly softened, about 2 minutes.

Add broth and ¼ cup water; bring to boil. Reduce heat, cover and simmer just until sweet potatoes are tender, about 6 minutes. Add zucchini, red pepper and remaining pepper and salt; cook, stirring, until zucchini is tender, about 3 minutes. Stir in lemon juice. Transfer to platter; add pork.

GARLIC YOGURT SAUCE Stir together yogurt and garlic; serve with pork and vegetables.

NUTRITIONAL INFORMATION, PER SERVING: about 293 cal, 31 g pro, 5 g total fat (1 g sat. fat), 32 g carb (5 g dietary fibre, 13 g sugar), 62 mg chol, 309 mg sodium, 984 mg potassium. % RDI: 10% calcium, 21% iron, 174% vit A, 125% vit C, 24% folate.

TIP FROM THE TEST KITCHEN

Pork tenderloin is a Test Kitchen favourite,— it cooks quickly, and one tenderloin is usually about the right size for four servings.

Curried Pork Tenderloin
WITH ALOO GOBI CAKES

HANDS-ON TIME	TOTAL TIME	MAKES
30 MINUTES	30 MINUTES	4 SERVINGS

ALOO GOBI CAKES In steamer basket set over saucepan of boiling water, steam potatoes, covered, for 5 minutes. Add cauliflower; steam until tender, about 5 minutes.

Meanwhile, in large nonstick skillet, heat half of the oil over medium-high heat; cook onion, stirring, until softened, about 4 minutes. Add garlic; cook, stirring, for 1 minute. Add cumin, coriander, curry powder, turmeric, salt and pepper; cook, stirring, until fragrant, about 2 minutes. Add potatoes and cauliflower; cook, stirring, for 1 minute.

In food processor, pulse together potato mixture, egg and lemon juice until in coarse crumbs.

In same skillet, heat remaining oil over medium heat. Working in batches, drop potato mixture by scant ⅓ cup, flattening to ½-inch thickness with spatula; cook, turning once, until crisp and golden, about 6 minutes. Transfer to plate; keep warm.

CURRIED PORK TENDERLOIN While potatoes are steaming, sprinkle pork with salt; rub curry paste all over pork.

In cast-iron or ovenproof skillet, heat oil over medium-high heat; cook pork, turning, until browned all over, about 5 minutes. Transfer to 425°F oven; bake until instant-read thermometer inserted into thickest part of pork reads 160°F or juices run clear when pork is pierced and just a hint of pink remains inside, about 12 minutes. Transfer to cutting board; tent with foil and let stand for 3 minutes before slicing crosswise. Serve with cakes.

NUTRITIONAL INFORMATION, PER SERVING: about 267 cal, 29 g pro, 9 g total fat (2 g sat. fat), 17 g carb (3 g dietary fibre, 3 g sugar), 109 mg chol, 328 mg sodium, 674 mg potassium. % RDI: 4% calcium, 16% iron, 3% vit A, 47% vit C, 19% folate.

ALOO GOBI CAKES

250 g	yellow-fleshed potatoes, peeled and cut in ¾-inch chunks
2 cups	small cauliflower florets
2 tsp	olive oil
1	onion, chopped
2	cloves garlic, chopped
¾ tsp	ground cumin
½ tsp	each ground coriander, curry powder and turmeric
¼ tsp	each salt and pepper
1	egg
1 tbsp	lemon juice

CURRIED PORK TENDERLOIN

1	pork tenderloin (about 450 g), trimmed
pinch	salt
1 tbsp	mild Indian curry paste
1 tsp	olive oil

Smoky Pork Bolognese Sauce

HANDS-ON TIME	TOTAL TIME	MAKES
15 MINUTES	1½ HOURS	ABOUT 7 CUPS

450 g	lean ground pork
2	strips bacon, chopped
2	carrots, diced
2	ribs celery, diced
1	onion, diced
3	cloves garlic, minced
4 cups	plain tomato sauce
1 cup	dry red wine
1 tsp	granulated sugar
1 tsp	dried oregano
¼ tsp	hot pepper flakes
1	bay leaf
¼ cup	chopped fresh parsley

In Dutch oven or large heavy-bottomed saucepan, cook pork and bacon over medium-high heat, breaking up pork with spoon, until pork is no longer pink, about 7 minutes. Using slotted spoon, transfer to bowl. Set aside. Drain all but 2 tbsp fat from pan.

Add carrots, celery and onion to pan; cook over medium heat, stirring occasionally, until softened, about 10 minutes. Add garlic; cook, stirring, until fragrant, about 1 minute.

Stir in pork mixture, tomato sauce, wine, sugar, oregano, hot pepper flakes and bay leaf. Bring to boil; reduce heat, cover and simmer, stirring occasionally, until slightly thickened, about 1 hour. Discard bay leaf. Stir in parsley. *(Make-ahead: Let cool; refrigerate in airtight container for up to 2 days or freeze for up to 2 months.)*

NUTRITIONAL INFORMATION, PER ½ CUP: about 135 cal, 8 g pro, 8 g total fat (2 g sat. fat), 8 g carb (2 g dietary fibre, 4 g sugar), 22 mg chol, 148 mg sodium, 433 mg potassium. % RDI: 3% calcium, 7% iron, 27% vit A, 23% vit C, 8% folate.

TIP FROM THE TEST KITCHEN
This recipe is easy to customize to make your own secret pasta sauce. Try adding mushrooms, peppers or olives, using a mix of ground beef and pork or stirring in fresh herbs. For an even richer smoked flavour, use double-smoked bacon.

Slow Cooker Lamb Shoulder
WITH LEMON AND HONEY

HANDS-ON TIME	TOTAL TIME	MAKES
10 MINUTES	7¼ HOURS	8 SERVINGS

Combine garlic, rosemary, lemon zest, salt and pepper; rub all over lamb. Place in slow cooker.

Whisk lemon juice with honey; pour over lamb. Add shallots. Cover and cook on low until lamb is tender, 7 to 8 hours.

Transfer lamb to cutting board; tent with foil and let stand for 10 minutes before slicing.

While lamb is resting, skim fat from cooking liquid. Whisk cornstarch with 2 tsp water; whisk into slow cooker. Cover and cook on high until thickened, about 10 minutes. Serve with lamb.

3	cloves garlic, thinly sliced
1 tbsp	chopped fresh rosemary
1 tsp	grated lemon zest
½ tsp	each salt and pepper
1.25 kg	boneless lamb shoulder roast
3 tbsp	lemon juice
1 tbsp	liquid honey
6	shallots, quartered
2 tsp	cornstarch

NUTRITIONAL INFORMATION, PER SERVING: about 240 cal, 31 g pro, 11 g total fat (4 g sat. fat), 5 g carb (trace dietary fibre, 3 g sugar), 76 mg chol, 241 mg sodium, 435 mg potassium. % RDI: 3% calcium, 14% iron, 1% vit A, 3% vit C, 28% folate.

TIP FROM THE TEST KITCHEN
Flavourful lamb shoulder, like other less tender (and often cheaper) cuts, benefits from long, slow cooking.

Moroccan Lamb Shank Soup

HANDS-ON TIME	TOTAL TIME	MAKES
55 MINUTES	3 HOURS	6 TO 8 SERVINGS

¼ tsp	each ground cumin, ground coriander, ground ginger and turmeric
¼ tsp	each salt and pepper
2	lamb shanks (about 780 g total), trimmed
1 tbsp	olive oil
2	onions, diced
2	carrots, diced
3	cloves garlic, minced
1	pkg (900 mL) sodium-reduced beef broth
1 tbsp	tomato paste
1	cinnamon stick
1	bay leaf
1	sweet red pepper, chopped
1	zucchini, chopped
2 tbsp	chopped fresh parsley

In large bowl, stir together cumin, coriander, ginger, turmeric, salt and pepper. Add lamb; rub cumin mixture all over lamb to coat. Set aside.

In Dutch oven or large heavy-bottomed saucepan, heat 2 tsp of the oil over medium heat; cook onions and carrots, stirring occasionally, until beginning to soften, about 6 minutes. Add garlic; cook, stirring often, for 3 minutes. Scrape into bowl.

In same pan, heat remaining oil over medium heat; cook lamb, turning occasionally, until browned all over, about 6 minutes. Add onion mixture, broth, tomato paste, cinnamon stick, bay leaf and 2 cups water; bring to boil. Reduce heat, cover and simmer, turning lamb once, until lamb is fork-tender, about 2 hours.

Transfer lamb to plate. Let cool enough to handle. Remove meat from bones; discard bones and any remaining fat.

While lamb is cooling, skim fat from surface of soup; discard cinnamon stick and bay leaf. Add red pepper and zucchini; cook, stirring occasionally, until tender, about 20 minutes.

Return lamb to soup; cook until heated through, about 2 minutes. Stir in parsley.

NUTRITIONAL INFORMATION, PER EACH OF 8 SERVINGS: about 116 cal, 11 g pro, 5 g total fat (2 g sat. fat), 7 g carb (2 g dietary fibre, 4 g sugar), 22 mg chol, 416 mg sodium, 290 mg potassium. % RDI: 3% calcium, 8% iron, 39% vit A, 52% vit C, 16% folate.

Lamb Chops
WITH MINT GREMOLATA & MINI POTATOES

HANDS-ON TIME 25 MINUTES	TOTAL TIME 25 MINUTES	MAKES 4 SERVINGS

MINI POTATOES In large saucepan of boiling salted water, cook potatoes until tender, about 15 minutes; drain. Transfer to bowl; toss with lemon zest, olive oil, salt and pepper.

MINT GREMOLATA Meanwhile, in bowl, whisk together mint, garlic, olive oil, lemon zest, salt and pepper; set aside.

LAMB CHOPS Rub lamb chops with olive oil; sprinkle with salt and pepper. In large skillet over medium heat, cook lamb chops until golden brown and instant-read thermometer inserted in centre reads 145°F for medium-rare, about 8 minutes. Top lamb with gremolata; serve with potatoes.

NUTRITIONAL INFORMATION, PER SERVING: about 290 cal, 14 g pro, 14 g total fat (3 g sat. fat), 29 g carb (3 g dietary fibre, 1 g sugar), 26 mg chol, 382 mg sodium, 692 mg potassium. % RDI: 32% calcium, 16% iron, 1% vit A, 35% vit C, 11% folate.

MINI POTATOES

1	bag (680 g) yellow-fleshed mini potatoes, scrubbed
1 tsp	grated lemon zest
1 tsp	extra-virgin olive oil
pinch	each salt and pepper

MINT GREMOLATA

2 tbsp	finely chopped fresh mint
2	cloves garlic, minced
2 tbsp	extra-virgin olive oil
1 tbsp	grated lemon zest
pinch	each salt and pepper

LAMB CHOPS

8	frenched lamb chops (about 450 g total), trimmed
1 tsp	extra-virgin olive oil
pinch	each salt and pepper

TIP FROM THE TEST KITCHEN
To store fresh herbs, wrap them in a damp paper towel and place in a plastic bag before refrigerating them.

Garlic Lemon Chicken

HANDS-ON TIME 20 MINUTES	TOTAL TIME 1 HOUR	MAKES 8 SERVINGS

1.75 kg	chicken pieces
1 tbsp	vegetable oil
1	lemon, cut in wedges
¼ cup	lemon juice
20	cloves garlic, peeled
2 tbsp	chopped fresh oregano (or 1 tsp dried)
½ tsp	each salt and pepper
1 tbsp	chopped fresh parsley

Cut any large chicken pieces in half. In large nonstick skillet, heat oil over medium-high heat. Working in batches, brown chicken, about 5 minutes. Drain off fat.

Arrange chicken and lemon wedges in 13- x 9-inch baking dish. Sprinkle with lemon juice, garlic, oregano, salt and pepper.

Bake in 425°F oven, turning and basting twice, until breasts are no longer pink inside and juices run clear when thickest parts of thighs are pierced, about 30 minutes. *(Make-ahead: Let cool for 30 minutes. Refrigerate until cold. Cover with foil and refrigerate for up to 1 day. Reheat, covered, in 375°F oven, basting once, for 15 minutes.)* Sprinkle with parsley.

NUTRITIONAL INFORMATION, PER SERVING: about 237 cal, 24 g pro, 14 g total fat (3 g sat. fat), 3 g carb (trace dietary fibre), 77 mg chol, 217 mg sodium. % RDI: 3% calcium, 9% iron, 4% vit A, 8% vit C, 3% folate.

TIP FROM THE TEST KITCHEN
If you're making this dish ahead or anticipate having leftovers, use chicken thighs and drumsticks—they stay moist when reheated.

Crispy Chicken
WITH HERB & WHEAT BERRY SALAD

HANDS-ON TIME	TOTAL TIME	MAKES
20 MINUTES	45 MINUTES	6 SERVINGS

HERB AND WHEAT BERRY SALAD In large saucepan of boiling water, cook wheat berries according to package instructions. Drain and rinse with cold water until cool; drain again.

In large bowl, combine wheat berries, cilantro, parsley, mint, green onions, tomatoes and cucumber. Whisk together oil, lemon zest, lemon juice, sumac, salt and pepper; drizzle over salad. Toss to coat.

CRISPY CHICKEN While wheat berries are cooking, sprinkle chicken all over with sumac, salt and pepper. In large ovenproof skillet, heat oil over medium-high heat; cook chicken, turning once, until golden, about 8 minutes. Transfer to plate, skin side up. Drain fat from pan.

Return chicken to pan, skin side up. Bake in 400°F oven until juices run clear when thickest part is pierced, about 18 minutes. Serve with salad.

NUTRITIONAL INFORMATION, PER SERVING: about 474 cal, 32 g pro, 30 g total fat (7 g sat. fat), 19 g carb (3 g dietary fibre, 3 g sugar), 116 mg chol, 327 mg sodium, 536 mg potassium. % RDI: 4% calcium, 26% iron, 15% vit A, 27% vit C, 17% folate.

HERB AND WHEAT BERRY SALAD

¾ cup	wheat berries, rinsed
1 cup	chopped fresh cilantro
½ cup	each chopped fresh parsley and fresh mint
3	green onions, chopped
2	plum tomatoes, seeded and chopped
1 cup	chopped English cucumber
3 tbsp	extra-virgin olive oil
½ tsp	grated lemon zest
3 tbsp	lemon juice
½ tsp	ground sumac
¼ tsp	each salt and pepper

CRISPY CHICKEN

675 g	bone-in skin-on chicken thighs
675 g	bone-in skin-on chicken drumsticks
½ tsp	ground sumac
¼ tsp	each salt and pepper
1 tsp	olive oil

TIP FROM THE TEST KITCHEN
Browning the chicken on the stovetop before finishing it in the oven makes the skin extra crispy. Instead of wheat berries, you can use barley, spelt berries or brown rice.

Healthy Baked Chicken Fingers

HANDS-ON TIME	TOTAL TIME	MAKES
10 MINUTES	30 MINUTES	8 SERVINGS

CHICKEN FINGERS

1 cup	natural (skin-on) almonds
1 tsp	smoked paprika
½ tsp	garlic powder
½ tsp	each salt and pepper
¼ cup	shelled hemp seeds
¼ cup	whole flaxseeds
2	eggs
845 g	boneless skinless chicken breasts, cut in 16 strips
	cooking spray

APRICOT MUSTARD SAUCE

½ cup	apricot jam
¼ cup	Dijon mustard

CHICKEN FINGERS In food processor, pulse together almonds, paprika, garlic powder, salt and pepper until coarsely ground. Transfer to shallow dish; stir in hemp seeds and flaxseeds.

In separate shallow dish, whisk eggs. Dip chicken in egg, letting excess drip back into dish; dredge in nut mixture, turning to coat. Place on parchment paper–lined rimmed baking sheet.

Mist chicken with cooking spray. Bake in 400°F oven, turning halfway through, until coating is golden and chicken is no longer pink inside, 15 to 20 minutes.

APRICOT MUSTARD SAUCE While chicken is baking, whisk jam with mustard. Serve with chicken strips.

NUTRITIONAL INFORMATION, PER SERVING: about 351 cal, 32 g pro, 17 g total fat (2 g sat. fat), 19 g carb (4 g dietary fibre, 14 g sugar), 109 mg chol, 329 mg sodium, 568 mg potassium. % RDI: 8% calcium, 17% iron, 5% vit A, 5% vit C, 13% folate.

VARIATION
Peanut Apricot Sauce

Substitute Apricot Mustard Sauce with Peanut Apricot Sauce. In microwaveable bowl, combine ¼ cup each apple juice and smooth peanut butter; 2 tbsp apricot jam; 1 clove garlic, minced; and 1½ tsp cider vinegar. Cover and microwave at medium-high (70%) for 2 minutes or until warm, stirring once.

Parmesan Chicken Tenders

HANDS-ON TIME	TOTAL TIME	MAKES
15 MINUTES	35 MINUTES	4 SERVINGS

Pour flour into shallow dish. In bowl, beat eggs. In another shallow dish, stir panko with Parmesan.

Sprinkle chicken with salt and pepper. One at a time, dip chicken strips into flour, shaking off excess; dip into eggs. Dredge in panko mixture, pressing to adhere.

Bake on parchment paper–lined baking sheet in 425°F oven until light golden and no longer pink inside, about 20 minutes.

NUTRITIONAL INFORMATION, PER SERVING: about 221 cal, 32 g pro, 6 g total fat (3 g sat. fat), 8 g carb (trace dietary fibre, trace sugar), 124 mg chol, 369 mg sodium, 362 mg potassium. % RDI: 10% calcium, 9% iron, 4% vit A, 2% vit C, 9% folate.

½ cup	all-purpose flour
2	eggs
1 cup	panko bread crumbs
½ cup	grated Parmesan cheese
450 g	chicken tenders
¼ tsp	each salt and pepper

SERVE WITH
Marinara Dipping Sauce

In saucepan, heat 1 tbsp olive oil over medium heat. Add 1 small onion, minced, and 1 clove garlic, minced; cook until softened, about 5 minutes. Stir in ¼ tsp dried Italian herb seasoning; cook until fragrant, about 30 seconds. Add ½ cup bottled strained tomatoes (passata) and ½ tsp liquid honey; cook, stirring, until thickened slightly, about 5 minutes. *(Make-ahead: Refrigerate in airtight container for up to 5 days or freeze for up to 1 month.)*

Easy Chicken Cordon Bleu
WITH ROASTED SWEET POTATO SALAD

HANDS-ON TIME 30 MINUTES	TOTAL TIME 30 MINUTES	MAKES 4 SERVINGS

ROASTED SWEET POTATO SALAD

1	large sweet potato (about 640 g), cut in ½-inch cubes
¼ cup	extra-virgin olive oil
2 tbsp	lime juice
1 tsp	liquid honey
pinch	each salt and pepper
4 cups	baby spinach

EASY CHICKEN CORDON BLEU

2	boneless skinless chicken breasts (about 450 g total)
pinch	each salt and pepper
4 tsp	Dijon mustard
2 tsp	chopped fresh thyme
2	slices Black Forest ham, halved
½ cup	shredded Swiss cheese

ROASTED SWEET POTATO SALAD Toss sweet potato with 1 tbsp of the oil; spread on lightly greased rimmed baking sheet. Bake in 400°F oven, turning occasionally, until tender and golden, about 20 minutes.

In bowl, whisk together remaining oil, the lime juice, honey, salt and pepper. Stir in sweet potato and spinach.

EASY CHICKEN CORDON BLEU Meanwhile, with knife parallel to cutting board, halve each chicken breast to form 2 thin cutlets (4 total). Sprinkle chicken with salt and pepper. Mix mustard with thyme; brush over tops of chicken. Wrap each cutlet with 1 slice of ham. Arrange, seam side down, on lightly greased rimmed baking sheet. Bake in 400°F oven until chicken is no longer pink inside, about 18 minutes. Sprinkle with Swiss; bake until melted, about 1 minute. Serve with salad.

NUTRITIONAL INFORMATION, PER SERVING: about 466 cal, 35 g pro, 20 g total fat (5 g sat. fat), 38 g carb (6 g dietary fibre, 15 g sugar), 82 mg chol, 314 mg sodium, 1,293 mg potassium. % RDI: 19% calcium, 19% iron, 339% vit A, 68% vit C, 33% folate.

TIP FROM THE TEST KITCHEN
At the grocery store, choose sweet potatoes with smooth skins and no blemishes or bruises. Store in a cool, dry place, but don't refrigerate.

Creamy Chicken & Green Bean Toss

HANDS-ON TIME	TOTAL TIME	MAKES
20 MINUTES	20 MINUTES	4 SERVINGS

In saucepan, cook couscous according to package instructions; drain and set aside.

In nonstick skillet, heat oil over medium heat; cook onion and garlic until onion is softened, about 2 minutes.

Sprinkle chicken with sumac, salt and pepper. Add to skillet and cook, stirring occasionally, until chicken is light golden and no longer pink inside, 8 minutes.

Meanwhile, in large saucepan of boiling water, cook green beans until tender-crisp, about 4 minutes.

Whisk together sour cream, half of the lemon juice and the mustard; add to skillet along with couscous and green beans, stirring until combined. Sprinkle with remaining lemon juice and the tarragon.

NUTRITIONAL INFORMATION, PER SERVING: about 279 cal, 20 g pro, 5 g total fat (1 g sat. fat), 39 g carb (3 g dietary fibre, 3 g sugar), 35 mg chol, 126 mg sodium, 391 mg potassium. % RDI: 7% calcium, 9% iron, 4% vit A, 13% vit C, 18% folate.

1 cup	Israeli (pearl) couscous
2 tsp	olive oil
1	small onion, sliced
2	cloves garlic, minced
225 g	boneless skinless chicken breast, cut in ¾-inch chunks
1½ tsp	sumac
pinch	each salt and pepper
225 g	green beans, trimmed
¼ cup	light sour cream
2 tbsp	lemon juice
2 tsp	grainy mustard
2 tbsp	chopped fresh tarragon

TIP FROM THE TEST KITCHEN
You'll find sumac, a tart and fruity Middle Eastern spice, in specialty stores and select grocery stores. If you can't find any, replace it with lemon pepper.

Chicken Tortilla Soup

HANDS-ON TIME 20 MINUTES	TOTAL TIME 40 MINUTES	MAKES 6 SERVINGS

3	boneless skinless chicken breasts (about 400 g total)
4	corn tortillas (about 4 inches)
2 tbsp	vegetable oil
1	onion, chopped
2	cloves garlic, minced
1 tsp	ground cumin
¼ tsp	chili powder
1	each sweet red and yellow pepper, chopped
4	plum tomatoes, chopped
4 cups	chicken broth
1 cup	corn kernels
1 tbsp	lime juice
¼ cup	chopped fresh cilantro

Cut chicken diagonally into ¼-inch thick strips; set aside.

Cut tortillas into ¼-inch thick strips. In large wide saucepan, heat 1 tsp of the oil over medium-high heat; cook tortilla strips, stirring, until crisp, about 2 minutes. Using slotted spoon, transfer to paper towels to drain.

Add remaining oil, the onion, garlic, cumin and chili powder to pan; cook over medium heat, stirring occasionally, until onion is softened, about 3 minutes.

Add chicken and red and yellow peppers; cook until chicken is golden, about 5 minutes. Add tomatoes and broth; bring to boil. Reduce heat and simmer for 7 minutes.

Add corn; cook for 2 minutes. Stir in lime juice. Ladle into bowls; top with tortilla chips and cilantro.

NUTRITIONAL INFORMATION, PER SERVING: about 207 cal, 21 g pro, 7 g total fat (1 g sat. fat), 16 g carb (2 g dietary fibre), 39 mg chol, 576 mg sodium. % RDI: 4% calcium, 11% iron, 12% vit A, 120% vit C, 16% folate.

TIP FROM THE TEST KITCHEN
Corn tortillas add authentic Mexican flavour, but you can also use flour tortillas. Top the soup with some diced avocado and a dollop of sour cream, if you like.

Chicken Skewers
WITH PEANUT LIME DIPPING SAUCE

HANDS-ON TIME	TOTAL TIME	MAKES
20 MINUTES	25 MINUTES	4 SERVINGS

Sprinkle chicken with salt and pepper. Thread onto metal or soaked wooden skewers. Arrange on lightly greased foil-lined baking sheet. Broil in oven until juices run clear when thickest part is pierced, about 6 minutes.

In small bowl, whisk together peanut butter, hoisin sauce, ginger, lime zest, lime juice and ¼ cup hot water. Serve with chicken.

NUTRITIONAL INFORMATION, PER SERVING: about 249 cal, 24 g pro, 14 g total fat (3 g sat. fat), 8 g carb (1 g dietary fibre, 4 g sugar), 75 mg chol, 267 mg sodium, 285 mg potassium. % RDI: 2% calcium, 11% iron, 2% vit A, 3% vit C, 9% folate.

450 g	boneless skinless chicken thighs, cut in 1-inch cubes
pinch	each salt and pepper
¼ cup	smooth peanut butter
2 tbsp	hoisin sauce
1 tbsp	grated fresh ginger
1 tsp	finely grated lime zest
1 tbsp	lime juice

SERVE WITH
Sautéed Garlic Swiss Chard

Trim and coarsely chop 500 g (about 1 bunch) Swiss chard. In large saucepan of salted boiling water, cover and cook Swiss chard until tender-crisp, 2 to 4 minutes. Drain, squeezing out excess liquid. Pat dry. *(Make-ahead: Refrigerate in airtight container for up to 24 hours.)*

In skillet, heat 1½ tbsp olive oil over medium-high-heat; cook 1 clove garlic, minced, and pinch each salt and hot pepper flakes, stirring, until garlic is golden, about 30 seconds. Add Swiss chard; cook, tossing, until heated through, 3 to 5 minutes.

Quick Chicken Cauliflower Curry

HANDS-ON TIME 30 MINUTES	TOTAL TIME 30 MINUTES	MAKES 4 SERVINGS

1 cup	basmati rice, rinsed
4 tsp	vegetable oil
450 g	boneless skinless chicken breasts, cut in ¾-inch pieces
pinch	each salt and pepper
6	cloves garlic, minced
4 tsp	minced fresh ginger
1	onion, chopped
4 tsp	mild Indian curry paste
4 cups	cauliflower florets (¾-inch pieces)
2 cups	sodium-reduced chicken broth
1 tbsp	sodium-reduced soy sauce
3 tbsp	all-purpose flour
1	sweet red pepper, cut in ¾-inch pieces
½ cup	frozen peas

Cook rice according to package instructions.

In large nonstick skillet, heat 1 tsp of the oil over medium-high heat; sauté chicken, salt and pepper until chicken is golden, about 4 minutes. Transfer to plate.

In same pan, heat remaining oil over medium-high heat; sauté garlic and ginger until fragrant, about 30 seconds. Stir in onion and curry paste; sauté until onion is softened, about 3 minutes. Stir in cauliflower, broth, soy sauce and ½ cup water; bring to boil. Reduce heat and simmer, stirring occasionally, until cauliflower is just tender, about 5 minutes.

Whisk flour with ¼ cup water; stir into curry mixture along with chicken and any juices, the red pepper and peas. Bring to boil; reduce heat to medium and simmer, stirring occasionally, until thickened and pepper is softened, about 4 minutes. Serve over rice.

NUTRITIONAL INFORMATION, PER SERVING: about 456 cal, 35 g pro, 10 g total fat (1 g sat. fat), 55 g carb (5 g dietary fibre, 6 g sugar), 65 mg chol, 678 mg sodium, 664 mg potassium. % RDI: 6% calcium, 14% iron, 12% vit A, 162% vit C, 35% folate.

TIP FROM THE TEST KITCHEN
Mild curry paste makes this dish appealing to kids who don't like spicy foods, but you can also use medium or hot paste for more kick.

Chicken Ratatouille
WITH LEMONY BASIL POLENTA

HANDS-ON TIME	TOTAL TIME	MAKES
30 MINUTES	30 MINUTES	4 SERVINGS

CHICKEN RATATOUILLE Sprinkle chicken with half of the oregano. In Dutch oven or large heavy-bottomed saucepan, heat 1 tsp of the oil over medium heat; cook chicken until golden, about 5 minutes. Using slotted spoon, transfer to plate.

Add remaining oil to pan; cook eggplant and onion, stirring frequently, until beginning to soften, about 5 minutes. Stir in zucchini, red pepper and garlic; cook, stirring occasionally, until tender-crisp, about 4 minutes.

Stir in tomatoes, pepper, hot pepper flakes, salt and remaining oregano. Return chicken to pan; cook, stirring occasionally, until vegetables are tender and juices run clear when thickest part of chicken is pierced, about 10 minutes.

LEMONY BASIL POLENTA Meanwhile, in saucepan, heat oil over medium heat; cook onion and garlic, stirring occasionally, until softened, about 5 minutes.

Add broth, ⅓ cup water, the pepper and salt; bring to boil. Reduce heat to medium-low. Gradually whisk in cornmeal; cook, stirring often, until polenta is thick enough to mound on spoon, 5 to 10 minutes. Stir in lemon zest, lemon juice and butter. Fold in basil. Serve topped with ratatouille.

NUTRITIONAL INFORMATION, PER SERVING: about 405 cal, 27 g pro, 17 g total fat (5 g sat. fat), 36 g carb (5 g dietary fibre, 8 g sugar), 102 mg chol, 264 mg sodium, 819 mg potassium. % RDI: 7% calcium, 24% iron, 21% vit A, 122% vit C, 31% folate.

CHICKEN RATATOUILLE

450 g	boneless skinless chicken thighs, quartered
1 tsp	dried oregano
2 tbsp	olive oil
1	Asian eggplant, thinly sliced
half	onion, thinly sliced
1	zucchini, thinly sliced
1	sweet red pepper, chopped
3	cloves garlic, minced
1	can (400 mL) diced tomatoes
½ tsp	pepper
¼ tsp	hot pepper flakes
pinch	salt

LEMONY BASIL POLENTA

1 tsp	olive oil
half	onion, diced
3	cloves garlic, minced
2 cups	no-salt-added chicken broth
¼ tsp	pepper
pinch	salt
¾ cup	cornmeal
1 tsp	grated lemon zest
1 tbsp	lemon juice
1 tbsp	unsalted butter
¼ cup	torn basil leaves

Mini Turkey Meat Loaves
WITH HERBED POTATOES

HANDS-ON TIME 20 MINUTES	TOTAL TIME 30 MINUTES	MAKES 4 SERVINGS

1 tbsp	olive oil
1	sweet red pepper, finely chopped
2	cloves garlic, minced
1 tbsp	dried Italian herb seasoning
½ tsp	each salt and pepper
2 cups	chopped baby spinach
450 g	lean ground turkey
½ cup	quick-cooking (not instant) rolled oats
½ cup	bottled strained tomatoes (passata)
1 tbsp	cider vinegar
2 tsp	liquid honey
3	large red-skinned potatoes, scrubbed and cut in ½-inch chunks

In small skillet, heat 1 tsp of the oil over medium heat; cook red pepper, garlic, half of the Italian seasoning and a pinch each of the salt and pepper, stirring often, until red pepper is softened, about 4 minutes. Stir in spinach; cook until wilted and no liquid remains, about 2 minutes. Transfer to bowl; let cool slightly.

Mix turkey and oats into pepper mixture. Roll into 8 balls; place 1 in each well of nonstick muffin pan.

Stir together strained tomatoes, vinegar and honey; spoon over meat loaves. Bake in 400°F oven until instant-read thermometer inserted into several reads 165°F, about 12 minutes. Broil until sauce on top thickens, about 2 minutes.

Meanwhile, in nonstick skillet, heat remaining oil over medium-high heat; cook potatoes and remaining Italian seasoning, salt and pepper, stirring, until potatoes are lightly browned, about 5 minutes. Add ½ cup water; reduce heat, cover and simmer until no liquid remains and potatoes are almost tender, about 5 minutes. Uncover and cook, stirring, until potatoes are tender, about 5 minutes. Serve with meat loaves.

NUTRITIONAL INFORMATION, PER SERVING: about 404 cal, 26 g pro, 14 g total fat (3 g sat. fat), 44 g carb (5 g dietary fibre, 8 g sugar), 89 mg chol, 474 mg sodium, 1,219 mg potassium. % RDI: 7% calcium, 35% iron, 24% vit A, 130% vit C, 28% folate.

Roasted Trout
WITH GREMOLATA

HANDS-ON TIME	TOTAL TIME	MAKES
5 MINUTES	20 MINUTES	4 SERVINGS

GREMOLATA In small bowl, combine parsley, zest and garlic; set aside.

ROASTED TROUT In microwaveable bowl, combine onions, garlic, oil, salt and pepper; cover and microwave on high, stirring twice, until softened, about 5 minutes.

Spread onion mixture in 13- x 9-inch baking dish. Arrange fish over top; sprinkle with gremolata.

Bake fish on bottom rack of 425°F oven until fish flakes easily when tested, about 10 minutes.

NUTRITIONAL INFORMATION, PER SERVING: about 281 cal, 33 g pro, 13 g total fat (3 g sat. fat), 6 g carb (1 g dietary fibre), 90 mg chol, 347 mg sodium. % RDI: 12% calcium, 6% iron, 13% vit A, 22% vit C, 20% folate.

GREMOLATA

¼ cup	finely chopped fresh parsley
2 tsp	grated lemon zest
1	clove garlic, minced

ROASTED TROUT

2 cups	thinly sliced onions
2	cloves garlic, minced
1 tbsp	olive oil
½ tsp	each salt and pepper
4	trout or salmon fillets (about 450 g total)

TIP FROM THE TEST KITCHEN
Gremolata is a versatile herb condiment that's traditionally served with osso buco. It's also delicious with grilled chicken, braised meats and seafood.

Tilapia & Red Pepper Fajitas

HANDS-ON TIME 25 MINUTES	TOTAL TIME 25 MINUTES	MAKES 4 SERVINGS

½ tsp	each smoked paprika and chili powder
¼ tsp	ground cumin
pinch	pepper
3	tilapia fillets (about 300 g total)
4 tsp	canola oil
1	onion, thinly sliced
1	sweet red pepper, thinly sliced
1 cup	rinsed drained canned black beans
½ cup	frozen corn kernels
2 tsp	lime juice
8	small soft flour tortillas (6 inches), warmed
⅓ cup	chopped fresh cilantro
⅓ cup	sour cream

Mix together paprika, chili powder, cumin and pepper; rub all over fish.

In nonstick skillet, heat half of the oil over medium heat; cook fish, turning once, until it flakes easily when tested, 8 to 10 minutes. Let cool enough to handle; break into bite-size pieces.

Meanwhile, add remaining oil to pan; cook onion and red pepper over medium heat, stirring occasionally, until onion is golden, about 8 minutes.

Stir in beans and corn; cook, stirring often, until corn is heated through, about 3 minutes. Stir in fish and lime juice. Scrape into serving dish; serve with tortillas, cilantro and sour cream.

NUTRITIONAL INFORMATION, PER SERVING: about 395 cal, 25 g pro, 13 g total fat (3 g sat. fat), 47 g carb (6 g dietary fibre, 4 g sugar), 44 mg chol, 577 mg sodium, 639 mg potassium. % RDI: 6% calcium, 24% iron, 14% vit A, 88% vit C, 55% folate.

VARIATION
Shrimp & Red Pepper Fajitas
Replace tilapia fillets with 300 g large shrimp (31 to 40 count), peeled and deveined. Add to skillet along with corn. Cook until shrimp are pink and opaque throughout, about 6 minutes.

Crispy Tilapia
WITH LEMON-HERB MAYO & OVEN FRIES

HANDS-ON TIME	TOTAL TIME	MAKES
30 MINUTES	30 MINUTES	4 SERVINGS

OVEN FRIES On lightly greased rimmed baking sheet, toss together potatoes, oil, salt and pepper. Bake in 425°F oven, turning once, until potatoes are golden and tender, about 25 minutes.

CRISPY TILAPIA While potatoes are roasting, in shallow dish, stir together cornmeal, chili powder and parsley. Sprinkle fish with salt and pepper; dredge in cornmeal mixture, turning to coat.

In nonstick skillet, heat half of the oil over medium heat; cook half of the fish, turning once, until it flakes easily when tested, about 8 minutes. Repeat with remaining oil and fish.

LEMON-HERB MAYO While fish is cooking, in small bowl, stir together mayonnaise, parsley, lemon juice and garlic. Serve with fish and oven fries.

NUTRITIONAL INFORMATION, PER SERVING: about 455 cal, 26 g pro, 26 g total fat (4 g sat. fat), 31 g carb (3 g dietary fibre, 2 g sugar), 63 mg chol, 325 mg sodium, 1,025 mg potassium. % RDI: 3% calcium, 16% iron, 4% vit A, 23% vit C, 29% folate.

TIP FROM THE TEST KITCHEN
Set the first batch of cooked fish on a rack while you're frying the second batch. This prevents the coating from becoming soggy.

OVEN FRIES

4	small yellow-fleshed potatoes (about 600 g total), cut in ¾-inch thick wedges
2 tsp	olive oil
pinch	each salt and pepper

CRISPY TILAPIA

¼ cup	cornmeal
1½ tsp	each chili powder and dried parsley
4	tilapia fillets (about 450 g total)
¼ tsp	each salt and pepper
2 tbsp	olive oil

LEMON-HERB MAYO

⅓ cup	mayonnaise
1 tbsp	chopped fresh parsley
2 tsp	lemon juice
1	small clove garlic, finely grated or pressed

Lemony Salmon & Quinoa Toss

HANDS-ON TIME 20 MINUTES	TOTAL TIME 20 MINUTES	MAKES 4 SERVINGS

1 cup	quinoa, rinsed
1 cup	sodium-reduced vegetable broth
½ tsp	salt
¼ cup	chopped fresh parsley
350 g	skinless salmon fillet, cut in 1-inch cubes
¼ tsp	pepper
½ tsp	olive oil
1	leek (white and light green parts only), halved lengthwise and thinly sliced crosswise
1	pkg (142 g) baby spinach
1 tbsp	grated lemon zest
¼ cup	lemon juice
1 tbsp	each liquid honey and Dijon mustard

In saucepan, bring quinoa, broth, half of the salt and 1 cup water to boil over high heat; reduce heat, cover and simmer until quinoa is tender and no liquid remains, about 15 minutes. Remove from heat; stir in parsley.

Meanwhile, sprinkle fish with pepper and remaining salt. In large nonstick skillet, heat oil over medium-high heat; cook fish, stirring often, until golden, about 5 minutes. Using slotted spoon, transfer fish to plate.

In same skillet, cook leek, stirring occasionally, until softened, about 4 minutes. Add spinach, lemon zest, lemon juice, honey and mustard; cook, stirring occasionally, until spinach is wilted, about 2 minutes.

Stir half of the spinach mixture into quinoa. Add fish to remaining spinach mixture, stirring to coat; serve over quinoa mixture.

NUTRITIONAL INFORMATION, PER SERVING: about 391 cal, 25 g pro, 15 g total fat (3 g sat. fat), 39 g carb (6 g dietary fibre, 7 g sugar), 48 mg chol, 568 mg sodium, 807 mg potassium. % RDI: 10% calcium, 31% iron, 43% vit A, 32% vit C, 55% folate.

TIP FROM THE TEST KITCHEN
Leeks are grown in sandy soil, and they may have some grit or sand between the inner layers. If so, place the sliced leeks in a colander, rinse and drain well.

Potato Salmon Cakes
WITH LEMON MUSTARD SAUCE

HANDS-ON TIME	TOTAL TIME	MAKES
35 MINUTES	1 HOUR	6 SERVINGS

POTATO SALMON CAKES Place fish on parchment paper–lined baking sheet; sprinkle with salt. Bake in 350°F oven until fish flakes easily when tested, 12 to 15 minutes. Break into bite-size pieces.

In large bowl, stir together egg, garlic, green onions, bread crumbs, chives, capers, mustard, lemon juice and pepper. Stir in mashed potatoes until well combined; gently fold in fish. Shape into twelve ½-inch thick patties; refrigerate for 15 minutes.

In large nonstick skillet, heat oil over medium heat. Cook patties, working in batches and turning once, until golden and hot in centre, 8 to 10 minutes. Serve with lemon wedges and lemon mustard sauce.

LEMON MUSTARD SAUCE While fish is baking, whisk together yogurt, mayonnaise, chives, mustard, lemon juice, salt and pepper; set aside.

NUTRITIONAL INFORMATION, PER SERVING: about 200 cal, 10 g pro, 12 g total fat (2 g sat. fat), 15 g carb (2 g dietary fibre, 2 g sugar), 49 mg chol, 368 mg sodium, 265 mg potassium. % RDI: 5% calcium, 7% iron, 4% vit A, 8% vit C, 13% folate.

TIP FROM THE TEST KITCHEN
If you don't have fresh salmon on hand, substitute 1 can (213 g) salmon, drained. Mash in the bones for extra calcium.

POTATO SALMON CAKES

170 g	skinless salmon fillet
pinch	salt
1	egg, lightly beaten
2	cloves garlic, minced
2	green onions, thinly sliced
½ cup	dried bread crumbs
2 tbsp	chopped fresh chives
1 tbsp	capers, drained, rinsed and chopped
1 tbsp	grainy mustard
2 tsp	lemon juice
pinch	pepper
2 cups	mashed potatoes
1 tbsp	olive oil
	lemon wedges

LEMON MUSTARD SAUCE

⅓ cup	2% plain Greek yogurt
¼ cup	light mayonnaise
2 tsp	chopped fresh chives
2 tsp	grainy mustard
2 tsp	lemon juice
pinch	each salt and pepper

White Fish Cakes
WITH LEMON-CHILI MAYO

HANDS-ON TIME	TOTAL TIME	MAKES
20 MINUTES	20 MINUTES	4 SERVINGS

WHITE FISH CAKES

1	rib celery, coarsely chopped
2	green onions, coarsely chopped
¼ cup	fresh parsley leaves
450 g	firm white-fleshed fish fillets (such as cod), coarsely chopped
¾ cup	fresh bread crumbs (about 1 slice bread)
1	egg
2 tsp	Dijon mustard
¼ tsp	pepper
1 tbsp	vegetable oil

LEMON-CHILI MAYO

⅓ cup	light mayonnaise
1½ tsp	lemon juice
¼ tsp	chili powder

WHITE FISH CAKES In food processor, pulse together celery, green onions and parsley until finely chopped. Scrape into bowl.

Add fish to food processor; pulse until fine but not puréed. Add to bowl; mix in bread crumbs, egg, mustard and pepper. Divide into 8 portions; form into ½-inch thick patties.

In nonstick skillet, heat oil over medium heat; cook fish cakes, turning once, until golden and hot in centre, 8 to 10 minutes.

LEMON-CHILI MAYO Meanwhile, whisk together mayonnaise, lemon juice and chili powder. Serve with fish cakes.

NUTRITIONAL INFORMATION, PER SERVING: about 268 cal, 26 g pro, 14 g total fat (2 g sat. fat), 7 g carb (1 g dietary fibre, 2 g sugar), 89 mg chol, 300 mg sodium, 619 mg potassium. % RDI: 8% calcium, 14% iron, 13% vit A, 10% vit C, 17% folate.

VARIATION
Cornmeal White Fish Cakes
Coat fish cakes in ⅓ cup medium- or fine-ground cornmeal. Cook as directed.

Buttery Halibut
WITH TOMATOES & ARUGULA SALAD

HANDS-ON TIME	TOTAL TIME	MAKES
15 MINUTES	15 MINUTES	4 SERVINGS

HALIBUT WITH TOMATOES In large nonstick skillet, heat 1 tbsp of the oil over medium heat; cook bread, stirring occasionally, until crisp and light golden, about 3 minutes. Scrape into bowl. Set aside.

In same pan, heat 2 tsp of the remaining oil over medium heat; cook tomatoes and garlic, stirring, until tomatoes are beginning to shrivel, about 2 minutes. Stir in vinegar and half each of the salt and pepper; cook, stirring, until fragrant, about 1 minute. Scrape into bowl with bread; toss to combine. Set aside.

Sprinkle fish with remaining salt and pepper. In same pan, heat remaining oil over medium-high heat; cook fish, turning once, until it is golden and flakes easily when tested, about 7 minutes. Add butter; cook, swirling pan, until butter is melted and fish is coated. Transfer to plate.

ARUGULA SALAD While fish is cooking, in large bowl, whisk together oil, lemon juice, honey, salt and pepper. Add arugula, Parmesan and red onion; toss to coat. Divide among serving plates; top with tomato mixture and fish.

NUTRITIONAL INFORMATION, PER SERVING: about 375 cal, 29 g pro, 21 g total fat (5 g sat. fat), 16 g carb (2 g dietary fibre, 5 g sugar), 48 mg chol, 453 mg sodium, 870 mg potassium. % RDI: 18% calcium, 17% iron, 22% vit A, 27% vit C, 34% folate.

HALIBUT WITH TOMATOES

2 tbsp	olive oil
1½ cups	cubed sourdough bread
1	pkg (255 g) cherry tomatoes
1	clove garlic, pressed or grated
2 tsp	balsamic vinegar
¼ tsp	each salt and pepper
4	skinless halibut fillets (about 450 g total)
1 tbsp	butter

ARUGULA SALAD

2 tbsp	olive oil
1 tbsp	lemon juice
½ tsp	liquid honey
pinch	each salt and pepper
6 cups	lightly packed baby arugula
⅓ cup	shaved Parmesan cheese
¼ cup	thinly sliced red onion

TIP FROM THE TEST KITCHEN
Instead of halibut, you can use any firm, white-fleshed fish, such as cod.

Seared Salmon
WITH MANGO SALSA & BUTTERY COUSCOUS

p.5

HANDS-ON TIME	TOTAL TIME	MAKES
15 MINUTES	15 MINUTES	4 SERVINGS

1 cup	Israeli (pearl) couscous
3	green onions, sliced
¼ cup	chopped fresh chives
4 tsp	butter
½ tsp	each salt and pepper
4	skinless salmon fillets (about 450 g total)
1 tsp	olive oil
1 cup	diced peeled mango
⅓ cup	diced red onion
3 tbsp	chopped fresh cilantro
½ tsp	grated lime zest
1 tbsp	lime juice
pinch	cayenne pepper

In saucepan, cook couscous according to package instructions. In large bowl, combine green onions, chives, butter and pinch each of the salt and pepper; stir in couscous until butter is melted. Keep warm.

While couscous is cooking, sprinkle fish with ¼ tsp each of the salt and pepper. In nonstick skillet, heat oil over medium heat; cook fish, turning once, until it flakes easily when tested, about 8 minutes.

In small bowl, stir together mango, red onion, cilantro, lime zest, lime juice, cayenne pepper and remaining salt and pepper.

Serve fish over couscous and top with mango mixture.

NUTRITIONAL INFORMATION, PER SERVING: about 399 cal, 25 g pro, 16 g total fat (5 g sat. fat), 37 g carb (2 g dietary fibre, 7 g sugar), 67 mg chol, 379 mg sodium, 544 mg potassium. % RDI: 4% calcium, 9% iron, 10% vit A, 32% vit C, 30% folate.

TIP FROM THE TEST KITCHEN
To dice a mango easily, peel it first, then cut slices off from each side of the large, flat pit. Be careful; ripe mangoes are very slippery.

Spicy Fish & Chorizo Stew

HANDS-ON TIME	TOTAL TIME	MAKES
30 MINUTES	30 MINUTES	4 SERVINGS

In large nonstick skillet, heat oil over medium heat; cook sausage, stirring often, until lightly browned, about 3 minutes. Add onion and hot pepper flakes; cook, stirring occasionally, until onion is softened, about 5 minutes.

Stir in tomato paste and garlic; cook, stirring, until fragrant, about 1 minute. Add tomatoes; bring to boil. Reduce heat and simmer, stirring occasionally, until beginning to thicken, about 8 minutes.

Add beans and salt; cook, stirring occasionally, until heated through and stew is slightly thickened, about 5 minutes. Stir in fish; simmer until fish flakes easily when tested, about 2 minutes. Remove from heat; gently stir in cilantro and vinegar.

NUTRITIONAL INFORMATION, PER SERVING: about 376 cal, 32 g pro, 13 g total fat (4 g sat. fat), 34 g carb (9 g dietary fibre, 8 g sugar), 61 mg chol, 645 mg sodium, 1,248 mg potassium. % RDI: 10% calcium, 49% iron, 22% vit A, 25% vit C, 12% folate.

2 tsp	olive oil
½ cup	diced dry-cured chorizo sausage
1	onion, diced
¼ tsp	hot pepper flakes
2 tbsp	tomato paste
4	cloves garlic, thinly sliced
1	can (796 mL) no-salt-added diced tomatoes
1	can (540 mL) no-salt-added white kidney beans, drained and rinsed
½ tsp	salt
340 g	skinless tilapia fillets or other white-fleshed fish, cut in 1-inch chunks
½ cup	chopped fresh cilantro
2 tsp	red wine vinegar

TIP FROM THE TEST KITCHEN
Canned tomatoes and beans add low-cost flavour to this satisfying stew, but they're typically high in sodium. Using no-salt-added varieties gives you much more control over how much salt goes into the dish.

Mini Fish Pies
WITH MASHED POTATO TOPPING

HANDS-ON TIME	TOTAL TIME	MAKES
20 MINUTES	30 MINUTES	4 SERVINGS

MINI FISH PIES

2 tsp	unsalted butter
2 cups	sliced leeks (white and light green parts only)
½ cup	diced carrot
½ cup	diced celery
3	cloves garlic, minced
2 tbsp	all-purpose flour
¾ cup	sodium-reduced vegetable broth
¼ cup	milk
300 g	cod fillets (or other firm white-fleshed fish), cut in 1-inch chunks
½ cup	frozen peas
2 tbsp	chopped fresh dill
4 tsp	lemon juice
2 tsp	Dijon mustard
¼ tsp	each salt and pepper

MASHED POTATO TOPPING

2	russet potatoes (about 500 g total)
¼ cup	milk
2 tsp	prepared horseradish
pinch	each salt and pepper

MINI FISH PIES In Dutch oven or large saucepan, melt butter over medium heat; cook leeks, carrot, celery and garlic, stirring occasionally, until beginning to soften, about 5 minutes.

Add flour; cook, stirring, for 1 minute. Whisk in broth and ¼ cup water; cook, whisking, until slightly thickened, about 2 minutes. Whisk in milk. Remove from heat; stir in fish, peas, dill, lemon juice, mustard, salt and pepper.

MASHED POTATO TOPPING Meanwhile, prick potatoes all over with fork. Microwave on high until fork-tender, about 7 minutes. Set aside until cool enough to handle. Peel potatoes; mash with milk, horseradish, salt and pepper.

Divide fish mixture among four 1-cup ramekins. Spoon potato mixture over each, smoothing tops. Bake on rimmed baking sheet in 425°F oven until filling is bubbly, about 10 minutes.

NUTRITIONAL INFORMATION, PER SERVING: about 257 cal, 19 g pro, 4 g total fat (2 g sat. fat), 38 g carb (4 g dietary fibre, 6 g sugar), 40 mg chol, 392 mg sodium, 1,000 mg potassium. % RDI: 11% calcium, 21% iron, 42% vit A, 47% vit C, 30% folate.

TIP FROM THE TEST KITCHEN

For a change, use sweet potatoes in this recipe instead of russets, following the same cooking instructions.

Snow Pea, Shrimp & Carrot Sauté

HANDS-ON TIME 15 MINUTES	TOTAL TIME 15 MINUTES	MAKES 4 SERVINGS

In large skillet, melt 2 tsp of the butter over medium-high heat; cook shrimp, stirring, until pink and opaque throughout, about 2 minutes. Transfer to plate.

Add remaining butter to pan; cook, stirring, until butter is fragrant and browned, about 1 minute. Stir in shallots and garlic; cook, stirring, until fragrant, about 1 minute.

Stir in carrots; cook, stirring, just until beginning to soften, about 2 minutes. Stir in snow peas; cook, stirring, until carrots and snow peas are tender-crisp, about 2 minutes. Stir in shrimp, salt and pepper. Serve with lemon wedges.

NUTRITIONAL INFORMATION, PER SERVING: about 183 cal, 19 g pro, 7 g total fat (4 g sat. fat), 10 g carb (3 g dietary fibre, 3 g sugar), 144 mg chol, 336 mg sodium, 394 mg potassium. % RDI: 8% calcium, 23% iron, 86% vit A, 40% vit C, 12% folate.

2 tbsp	butter
450 g	extra-jumbo shrimp (16 to 20 count), peeled and deveined
2	shallots, halved and thinly sliced
6	cloves garlic, minced
1	bunch carrots, halved lengthwise then cut diagonally in long, thin slices
3 cups	trimmed snow peas
¼ tsp	each salt and pepper
	lemon wedges

TIP FROM THE TEST KITCHEN
To trim snow peas, cut off the stem ends and pull off the fibrous strings that run along the outer edges of the pods.

Quick Shrimp Pilau

HANDS-ON TIME	TOTAL TIME	MAKES
15 MINUTES	30 MINUTES	4 SERVINGS

1 tbsp	butter
1	onion, chopped
2	cloves garlic, chopped
½ tsp	each ground coriander and ground cumin
¼ tsp	ground cloves
pinch	each turmeric, salt and pepper
1 cup	basmati rice, rinsed and drained
1	bay leaf
1 cup	sodium-reduced chicken broth
350 g	jumbo shrimp (21 to 25 count), peeled and deveined
2 tsp	vegetable oil
1 cup	frozen peas
⅓ cup	chopped fresh cilantro
1 tbsp	lime juice

In saucepan, melt butter over medium heat; cook onion and garlic, stirring often, until onion is softened, about 5 minutes. Stir in half each of the coriander and cumin, the cloves, turmeric, salt and pepper; cook, stirring, until fragrant, about 30 seconds. Stir in rice and bay leaf. Stir in broth and 1 cup water; bring to boil.

Reduce heat, cover and simmer until rice is tender and no liquid remains, about 12 minutes. Remove from heat. Let stand, covered, for 5 minutes; fluff with fork. Discard bay leaf.

Meanwhile, stir together shrimp and remaining coriander and cumin. In large skillet, heat oil over medium heat; cook shrimp and peas, stirring occasionally, until shrimp are pink and opaque throughout, about 5 minutes.

Add rice mixture, cilantro and lime juice; toss until combined.

NUTRITIONAL INFORMATION, PER SERVING: about 328 cal, 20 g pro, 7 g total fat (2 g sat. fat), 46 g carb (3 g dietary fibre, 3 g sugar), 107 mg chol, 293 mg sodium, 267 mg potassium. % RDI: 7% calcium, 19% iron, 13% vit A, 12% vit C, 15% folate.

VARIATION
Quick Chicken Pilau
Replace shrimp with 450 g boneless skinless chicken breasts or thighs, diced. Cook until chicken breasts are no longer pink inside or until juices run clear when thickest parts of thighs are pierced, 8 to 10 minutes.

Shrimp, Scallop &
Tomato Stew
WITH LEMONY ORZO

HANDS-ON TIME	TOTAL TIME	MAKES
30 MINUTES	30 MINUTES	4 SERVINGS

SHRIMP AND SCALLOP STEW In large nonstick skillet, heat oil over medium heat; cook leek, carrot and fennel, stirring occasionally, until softened and light golden, about 7 minutes. Stir in garlic, half each of the pepper and salt, the paprika, cumin and hot pepper flakes; cook, stirring, until fragrant, about 1 minute.

Stir in tomatoes and ½ cup water; bring to boil. Reduce heat and simmer, stirring occasionally, until thickened, 6 to 8 minutes.

Sprinkle shrimp and scallops with remaining pepper and salt. Stir into tomato mixture; cook, stirring occasionally, until shrimp are pink and scallops are opaque throughout, 5 to 7 minutes. Stir in parsley.

LEMONY ORZO Meanwhile, in large saucepan of boiling salted water, cook pasta according to package instructions; drain. Stir in lemon zest and juice. Serve with stew.

NUTRITIONAL INFORMATION, PER SERVING: about 342 cal, 25 g pro, 5 g total fat (1 g sat. fat), 51 g carb (5 g dietary fibre, 10 g sugar), 73 mg chol, 345 mg sodium, 944 mg potassium. % RDI: 17% calcium, 31% iron, 52% vit A, 43% vit C, 57% folate.

SHRIMP AND SCALLOP STEW

2 tsp	olive oil
1	leek (white and light green parts only), chopped
1	carrot, diced
half	bulb fennel, cored and chopped
3	cloves garlic, minced
½ tsp	pepper
¼ tsp	salt
¼ tsp	each smoked paprika and ground cumin
pinch	hot pepper flakes
1	can (796 mL) no-salt-added diced tomatoes
200 g	jumbo shrimp (21 to 25 count), peeled and deveined
200 g	sea scallops
2 tbsp	chopped fresh parsley

LEMONY ORZO

1 cup	orzo
½ tsp	grated lemon zest
1 tbsp	lemon juice

Hearty Red Lentil Curry
WITH EGGS

HANDS-ON TIME 20 MINUTES	TOTAL TIME 30 MINUTES	MAKES 4 SERVINGS

2 tbsp	olive oil
1	onion, finely chopped
1	large sweet potato (about 350 g), peeled and diced
4 cups	bite-size cauliflower florets (about half head)
2	cloves garlic, pressed or grated
1 tbsp	curry powder
2 tsp	grated fresh ginger
1 tsp	ground coriander
½ tsp	each ground cumin and turmeric
3 cups	sodium-reduced vegetable broth
1 cup	dried red lentils, rinsed
½ tsp	pepper
¼ tsp	salt
4	eggs
2 tbsp	chopped fresh cilantro

In Dutch oven or large heavy-bottomed saucepan, heat oil over medium heat; cook onion, sweet potato and cauliflower, stirring often, until slightly softened, about 6 minutes. Add garlic, curry powder, ginger, coriander, cumin and turmeric; cook, stirring, until fragrant, about 1 minute.

Stir in broth and lentils; bring to boil. Reduce heat, cover and simmer, stirring occasionally, until lentils and vegetables are tender and almost no liquid remains, about 10 minutes. Stir in pepper and salt.

Divide among 4 lightly greased 1½-cup ovenproof bowls. Using spoon, form well in centres; crack 1 egg into each. Bake on rimmed baking sheet in 425°F oven until egg whites are set yet yolks are still slightly runny, 10 to 12 minutes. Let stand for 2 minutes. Sprinkle with cilantro.

NUTRITIONAL INFORMATION, PER SERVING: about 396 cal, 22 g pro, 14 g total fat (3 g sat. fat), 49 g carb (12 g dietary fibre, 10 g sugar), 193 mg chol, 349 mg sodium, 925 mg potassium. % RDI: 11% calcium, 54% iron, 88% vit A, 90% vit C, 151% folate.

TIP FROM THE TEST KITCHEN
The eggs will continue to cook as they stand, so remove them from the oven just before they reach desired doneness to avoid overcooked yolks.

Tomato & Feta Baked Eggs

HANDS-ON TIME	TOTAL TIME	MAKES
25 MINUTES	45 MINUTES	4 TO 6 SERVINGS

In large skillet, heat oil over medium heat; cook onion and red pepper, stirring occasionally, until onion is softened and light golden, about 10 minutes.

Stir in garlic, cumin, paprika, half each of the salt and pepper, and the cayenne pepper; cook, stirring, until fragrant, about 30 seconds. Stir in tomatoes and tomato paste; bring to boil. Reduce heat and simmer, stirring occasionally, until thickened, about 10 minutes.

Scrape into 12-cup casserole dish; sprinkle with all but 2 tbsp of the feta. Using spoon, make 6 wells in tomato mixture; crack 1 egg into each well. Sprinkle remaining salt and pepper over eggs. Bake in 375°F oven until egg whites are set yet yolks are still slightly runny, 15 to 18 minutes.

Remove from oven; tent with foil and let stand for 5 minutes. Sprinkle with remaining feta and the parsley.

NUTRITIONAL INFORMATION, PER EACH OF 6 SERVINGS: about 157 cal, 9 g pro, 9 g total fat (3 g sat. fat), 11 g carb (2 g dietary fibre, 6 g sugar), 191 mg chol, 433 mg sodium, 458 mg potassium. % RDI: 11% calcium, 19% iron, 18% vit A, 65% vit C, 20% folate.

1 tbsp	olive oil
1	onion, sliced
half	sweet red pepper, diced
3	cloves garlic, minced
¼ tsp	ground cumin
¼ tsp	sweet paprika
¼ tsp	each salt and pepper
pinch	cayenne pepper
1	can (796 mL) diced tomatoes
3 tbsp	tomato paste
⅓ cup	crumbled feta cheese
6	eggs
2 tbsp	chopped fresh parsley

TIP FROM THE TEST KITCHEN
To avoid getting any bits of shell in the tomato mixture, crack each egg into a small bowl before tipping it into a well.

Green Onion & Tomato Frittata

HANDS-ON TIME 15 MINUTES	TOTAL TIME 30 MINUTES	MAKES 4 TO 6 SERVINGS

1	bunch green onions
8	eggs
½ tsp	salt
pinch	pepper
3 tbsp	olive oil
3 tbsp	finely diced pancetta or prosciutto (optional)
⅓ cup	grated Parmesan cheese
450 g	tomatoes, thinly sliced

Chop white and light green parts of green onions; thinly slice enough of the dark green parts to make 2 tbsp; set aside.

Using fork, whisk together eggs, salt, pepper and 2 tbsp water.

In large ovenproof skillet, heat oil over medium heat; cook white and light green parts of green onions and pancetta (if using), stirring, until green onions are softened, about 2 minutes.

Pour in egg mixture; cook, running spatula along edge to let egg mixture flow underneath, until about one-third of the mixture is still liquid. Sprinkle evenly with Parmesan. Overlap tomatoes on top.

Bake in top third of 425°F oven until set and light golden, about 12 minutes. Sprinkle with dark green parts of green onions.

NUTRITIONAL INFORMATION, PER EACH OF 6 SERVINGS: about 193 cal, 11 g pro, 15 g total fat (4 g sat. fat), 5 g carb (1 g dietary fibre, 3 g sugar), 251 mg chol, 350 mg sodium, 313 mg potassium. % RDI: 10% calcium, 9% iron, 17% vit A, 18% vit C, 22% folate.

TIP FROM THE TEST KITCHEN
To remove your frittata from the skillet, run a small knife around the edge to loosen it first. Using a large spatula, lift the frittata onto a cutting board to slice.

Pasta & Broccoli Frittata

HANDS-ON TIME	TOTAL TIME	MAKES
15 MINUTES	25 MINUTES	4 SERVINGS

In 9- or 10-inch nonstick ovenproof skillet, heat oil over medium heat; cook onion, carrot, garlic and herb seasoning, stirring often, until softened, 5 to 8 minutes.

In large bowl, whisk together eggs, milk, salt and pepper; add broccoli, pasta and hot pepper sauce. Pour into pan, stirring to combine; reduce heat to medium-low. Sprinkle with Parmesan; cook until bottom and side of frittata are firm yet top is still slightly runny, about 10 minutes. Broil until golden and set, 3 to 5 minutes. Cut into wedges.

NUTRITIONAL INFORMATION, PER SERVING: about 299 cal, 19 g pro, 16 g total fat (5 g sat. fat), 18 g carb (2 g dietary fibre), 380 mg chol, 625 mg sodium. % RDI: 19% calcium, 14% iron, 69% vit A, 22% vit C, 37% folate.

1 tbsp	vegetable oil
1	onion, sliced
1	carrot, thinly sliced
2	cloves garlic, minced
½ tsp	dried Italian herb seasoning
8	eggs
¼ cup	milk
½ tsp	salt
¼ tsp	pepper
1½ cups	frozen broccoli florets, thawed and patted dry
1 cup	cooked short pasta (¾ cup uncooked)
dash	hot pepper sauce
⅓ cup	grated Parmesan cheese

TIP FROM THE TEST KITCHEN

A frittata is a versatile, easy way to use leftover pasta or cooked vegetables.

Quick Egg & Veggie Fried Rice

HANDS-ON TIME	TOTAL TIME	MAKES
15 MINUTES	30 MINUTES	4 SERVINGS

2 tbsp	vegetable oil
3	green onions, thinly sliced (light and dark green parts separated)
1½ cup	sliced stemmed mushrooms, such as shiitake or cremini
1	carrot, diced
3	cloves garlic, minced
1 tbsp	minced fresh ginger
5 cups	cold cooked rice
½ cup	frozen peas
4	eggs, lightly beaten
2 tbsp	sodium-reduced soy sauce
1 tbsp	oyster sauce
2 tsp	sriracha or other Asian chili sauce
1 tsp	sesame oil

In wok or large nonstick skillet, heat vegetable oil over medium-high heat. Add light green parts of green onions; cook, stirring, until softened, about 1 minute.

Add mushrooms, carrot, garlic and ginger; cook, stirring, until softened, about 3 minutes.

Stir in rice and peas; cook, stirring frequently, until rice is hot, about 5 minutes. Push rice mixture into ring around edge of pan, leaving space in centre; pour eggs into centre. Cook, stirring eggs occasionally, until softly scrambled, about 2 minutes.

Stir rice mixture into eggs. Add soy sauce, oyster sauce, sriracha and sesame oil; cook, stirring, for 1 minute. Sprinkle with dark green parts of green onions.

NUTRITIONAL INFORMATION, PER SERVING: about 444 cal, 14 g pro, 14 g total fat (2 g sat. fat), 65 g carb (3 g dietary fibre, 3 g sugar), 183 mg chol, 542 mg sodium, 315 mg potassium. % RDI: 6% calcium, 14% iron, 46% vit A, 7% vit C, 25% folate.

TIP FROM THE TEST KITCHEN
For best results when making fried rice, use rice that has been cooked the day before and refrigerated; warm, freshly made rice becomes sticky and mushy when fried.

Eggs Poached In Tomato Fennel Sauce

HANDS-ON TIME	TOTAL TIME	MAKES
20 MINUTES	30 MINUTES	4 SERVINGS

In large skillet, heat oil over medium heat; cook fennel and ½ cup water, stirring occasionally, until fennel is softened and water has evaporated, about 15 minutes. Add white parts of green onions; cook, stirring, until softened, about 1 minute. Stir in tomato sauce, vinegar and sugar. Bring to boil; reduce heat to simmer.

Using back of spoon, make 4 wells in sauce; gently break 1 egg into each. Sprinkle with salt and pepper. Simmer, partially covered, until egg whites are set yet yolks are still slightly runny, about 9 minutes. Sprinkle with green parts of green onions.

NUTRITIONAL INFORMATION, PER SERVING: about 201 cal, 9 g pro, 13 g total fat (3 g sat. fat), 14 g carb (4 g dietary fibre, 9 g sugar), 193 mg chol, 247 mg sodium, 775 mg potassium. % RDI: 7% calcium, 14% iron, 24% vit A, 45% vit C, 28% folate.

2 tsp	olive oil
1	small bulb fennel, trimmed, cored and thinly sliced
2	green onions, sliced (white and light green parts separated)
2 cups	plain tomato sauce
1 tsp	sherry vinegar or red wine vinegar
½ tsp	granulated sugar
4	eggs
pinch	each salt and pepper

Scrambled Eggs
WITH SHRIMP

HANDS-ON TIME	TOTAL TIME	MAKES
10 MINUTES	15 MINUTES	4 SERVINGS

In large nonstick skillet, heat sesame oil over medium-high heat; cook shrimp, stirring often, until pink and opaque throughout, about 3 minutes. Keep warm.

Wipe pan clean; heat vegetable oil over medium heat. Cook eggs and three-quarters of the green onions, stirring, until creamy and just set, about 2 minutes. Gently fold in shrimp. Top with remaining green onions.

NUTRITIONAL INFORMATION, PER SERVING: about 281 cal, 28 g pro, 17 g total fat (4 g sat. fat), 2 g carb (trace dietary fibre, 1 g sugar), 554 mg chol, 252 mg sodium, 281 mg potassium. % RDI: 9% calcium, 24% iron, 28% vit A, 3% vit C, 35% folate.

1 tsp	sesame oil
340 g	extra-jumbo shrimp (16 to 20 count), peeled and deveined
2 tsp	vegetable oil
10	eggs, lightly beaten
2	green onions, thinly sliced

Roasted Peppers
WITH EGGS

HANDS-ON TIME 10 MINUTES	TOTAL TIME 30 MINUTES	MAKES 4 SERVINGS

2	large red peppers
⅓ cup	shredded Havarti cheese
2	green onions, thinly sliced (white and green parts separated)
4	eggs
pinch	each salt and pepper

Leaving stems intact, halve and core red peppers. Arrange, cut sides down, on foil-lined rimmed baking sheet. Bake in 425°F oven just until beginning to soften, about 10 minutes.

Turn red peppers cut sides up; sprinkle with one-quarter of the Havarti and the white parts of green onions. Crack 1 egg into each red pepper half; sprinkle with salt and pepper.

Bake in 425°F oven until egg whites are just set yet yolks are still runny, 8 to 10 minutes. Sprinkle with remaining Havarti and green parts of green onions. Broil until cheese is melted, about 1 minute.

NUTRITIONAL INFORMATION, PER SERVING: about 136 cal, 9 g pro, 9 g total fat (4 g sat. fat), 6 g carb (1 g dietary fibre, 4 g sugar), 194 mg chol, 136 mg sodium, 208 mg potassium. % RDI: 9% calcium, 9% iron, 35% vit A, 225% vit C, 20% folate.

SERVE WITH
Cucumber Cilantro Salad
In bowl, mix together ¼ cup diced red onion, 2 tbsp chopped fresh cilantro, 1 tbsp granulated sugar, 1 tbsp vinegar, ½ tsp sesame oil, ¼ tsp salt and pinch hot pepper flakes. Stir in 2½ cups diced English cucumber (about 1 cucumber).

Superfood Platter

HANDS-ON TIME	TOTAL TIME	MAKES
20 MINUTES	30 MINUTES	4 SERVINGS

In saucepan, bring 2 cups water to boil. Add quinoa; cover, reduce heat and simmer until no liquid remains and quinoa is tender, about 15 minutes. Remove from heat; let stand, covered, for 5 minutes. Fluff with fork. Transfer to platter; keep warm.

Meanwhile, in large skillet, heat oil over medium heat. Add onion, garlic, coriander and cumin; cook, stirring, until onion is softened, about 4 minutes. Add mushrooms; cook, stirring, until softened, about 4 minutes.

Add kale, red pepper, chickpeas, broth, salt and pepper; cook, stirring, just until kale is wilted and red pepper is tender-crisp, about 4 minutes. Stir in lemon juice.

Spoon kale mixture over quinoa; sprinkle with almonds.

NUTRITIONAL INFO, PER SERVING: about 337 cal, 14 g pro, 8 g total fat (1 g sat. fat), 57 g carb (11 g dietary fibre, 9 g sugar), 0 mg chol, 396 mg sodium, 1,141 mg potassium. % RDI: 20% calcium, 40% iron, 148% vit A, 260% vit C, 55% folate.

1 cup	quinoa, rinsed and drained
2 tsp	olive oil
1	small onion, finely chopped
3	cloves garlic, minced
2 tsp	each ground coriander and ground cumin
1	pkg (227 g) cremini mushrooms, sliced
6 cups	thinly sliced stemmed kale
1	sweet red pepper, diced
1 cup	rinsed drained canned chickpeas
½ cup	sodium-reduced vegetable broth
¼ tsp	each salt and pepper
1 tbsp	lemon juice
2 tbsp	sliced almonds, toasted

TIP FROM THE TEST KITCHEN

Quinoa is both a complete protein and a timesaver. It cooks quickly, like rice, and you can freeze cooled cooked quinoa for up to one month. Thaw to use in salads, soups, casseroles and stir-fries.

Vegetarian Tex-Mex Shepherd's Pie

HANDS-ON TIME 20 MINUTES	TOTAL TIME 1 HOUR	MAKES 4 TO 6 SERVINGS

6	yellow-fleshed potatoes (about 1 kg total)
¼ cup	milk
2 tbsp	chopped fresh parsley
2 tbsp	butter
¾ tsp	each salt and pepper
1 tbsp	vegetable oil
2	carrots, diced
1	each onion and sweet red pepper, chopped
1 tbsp	chili powder
½ tsp	ground cumin
pinch	cayenne pepper
¾ cup	bulgur
2 tbsp	all-purpose flour
1½ cups	vegetable broth
1 cup	corn kernels

Peel and cut potatoes into 2-inch chunks. In saucepan of boiling salted water, cover and cook potatoes until tender, about 20 minutes; drain and mash. Blend in milk, parsley, butter and ½ tsp each of the salt and pepper.

Meanwhile, in large skillet, heat oil over medium heat; cook carrots, onion, red pepper, chili powder, cumin and cayenne pepper, stirring occasionally, until onion is softened, about 5 minutes.

Add bulgur and flour; cook, stirring, for 1 minute. Gradually stir in broth; cover and cook over low heat until liquid is absorbed, about 10 minutes.

Add corn and remaining salt and pepper. Spread in 8-inch square baking dish; spread potatoes over top. Broil for 2 minutes or until golden. *(Make-ahead: Let cool for 30 minutes; refrigerate until cold. Cover and refrigerate for up to 24 hours; reheat, covered, in 350°F oven for 30 minutes or until filling is bubbly.)*

NUTRITIONAL INFORMATION, PER EACH OF 6 SERVINGS: about 277 cal, 7 g pro, 7 g total fat (3 g sat. fat), 50 g carb (6 g dietary fibre), 11 mg chol, 529 mg sodium. % RDI: 5% calcium, 14% iron, 78% vit A, 73% vit C, 19% folate.

Broiled Tofu
WITH NO-COOK PEANUT SAUCE

HANDS-ON TIME	TOTAL TIME	MAKES
15 MINUTES	25 MINUTES	4 SERVINGS

NO-COOK PEANUT SAUCE In small bowl, whisk together peanut butter, ginger, soy sauce, vinegar, sesame oil and chili paste; slowly whisk in ¼ cup hot water. Stir in onions. Set aside.

BROILED TOFU Using paper towels, pat tofu dry. Brush rimmed baking sheet with 1 tsp of the oil. Arrange tofu on baking sheet; brush remaining oil over top. Broil, about 8 inches from heat, until crisp and dry looking, about 15 minutes.

Meanwhile, in steamer, cover and steam broccoli until tender-crisp, about 3 minutes. Serve tofu over broccoli. Drizzle with peanut sauce; sprinkle with sesame seeds.

NUTRITIONAL INFORMATION, PER SERVING: about 347 cal, 22 g pro, 24 g total fat (3 g sat. fat), 15 g carb (4 g dietary fibre, 4 g sugar), 0 mg chol, 241 mg sodium, 461 mg potassium. % RDI: 21% calcium, 23% iron, 22% vit A, 73% vit C, 38% folate.

NO-COOK PEANUT SAUCE

¼ cup	reduced-fat peanut butter
1 tbsp	grated fresh ginger
2 tsp	each sodium-reduced soy sauce and rice vinegar
1 tsp	sesame oil
½ tsp	Asian chili paste (such as sambal oelek)
2	green onions, thinly sliced

BROILED TOFU

1	pkg (454 g) firm tofu, cut in 8 slices
2 tbsp	olive oil
1	large stalk broccoli, stems removed and separated in florets
1 tbsp	toasted sesame seeds

TIP FROM THE TEST KITCHEN
Don't like broccoli? Make this dish with red peppers, carrots, sugar snap peas or another vegetable instead.

Tofu & Fresh Vegetable Stir-Fry

HANDS-ON TIME	TOTAL TIME	MAKES
25 MINUTES	25 MINUTES	4 SERVINGS

3 tbsp	vegetable oil
1	pkg (350 g) extra-firm tofu, cut in ½-inch wide strips
⅔ cup	no-salt-added vegetable broth
1 tbsp	sodium-reduced soy sauce
1 tbsp	hoisin sauce
2 tsp	unseasoned rice vinegar
2 tsp	cornstarch
3	green onions, sliced (white and light green parts separated)
2	cloves garlic, minced
1 tbsp	minced fresh ginger
3 cups	sugar snap peas (about 250 g), trimmed
2 cups	sliced stemmed shiitake mushrooms (about 115 g)
3 cups	chopped napa cabbage
2 tsp	sesame oil

In wok or large nonstick skillet, heat 2 tbsp of the vegetable oil over medium-high heat; cook tofu, turning occasionally, until crisp and golden, about 8 minutes. Drain on paper towel–lined plate.

Meanwhile, in bowl, whisk together broth, soy sauce, hoisin sauce, vinegar and cornstarch; add enough water to make 1 cup. Set aside.

Heat remaining vegetable oil over medium-high heat; cook white parts of green onions, the garlic and ginger, stirring, for 1 minute. Stir in sugar snap peas and mushrooms; cook, stirring, for 3 minutes. Stir in cabbage; cook, stirring, for 1 minute. Stir in broth mixture and tofu; cook, stirring, until coated and sauce is slightly thickened, about 1 minute.

Stir in sesame oil and green parts of green onions.

NUTRITIONAL INFORMATION, PER SERVING: about 267 cal, 19 g pro, 17 g total fat (2 g sat. fat), 15 g carb (4 g dietary fibre, 5 g sugar), 0 mg chol, 246 mg sodium, 457 mg potassium. % RDI: 17% calcium, 24% iron, 8% vit A, 50% vit C, 28% folate.

TIP FROM THE TEST KITCHEN
Stir-fries cook very quickly, making them ideal for weeknight meals. Be sure to have all the ingredients measured and prepped before you start cooking.

FROM TOP:
EDAMAME–BLUEBERRY SALAD
WITH GRILLED CHICKEN
opposite

EDAMAME GUACAMOLE
p.106

Edamame-Blueberry Salad
WITH GRILLED HERB CHICKEN

HANDS-ON TIME	TOTAL TIME	MAKES
25 MINUTES	45 MINUTES	4 SERVINGS

LEMON-BASIL VINAIGRETTE In small bowl, whisk together lemon zest, lemon juice, basil, mustard, salt and pepper; slowly whisk in oil. Set aside.

SALAD Between plastic wrap, use meat mallet or heavy-bottomed saucepan to flatten chicken to ½-inch thickness.

Whisk together oil, thyme, tarragon, basil, salt and pepper; rub over chicken. Let stand for 30 minutes. *(Make-ahead: Refrigerate in airtight container for up to 24 hours.)*

Meanwhile, in saucepan of boiling salted water, cook edamame for 1 minute. Drain and let cool to room temperature.

Place chicken on greased grill over medium-high heat; close lid and grill, turning once, until no longer pink inside, about 8 minutes. Transfer to cutting board; slice.

In large bowl, toss together edamame, arugula, blueberries, pumpkin seeds and vinaigrette. Top with chicken.

NUTRITIONAL INFORMATION, PER SERVING: about 420 cal, 35 g pro, 26 g total fat (4 g sat. fat), 15 g carb (5 g dietary fibre, 6 g sugar), 165 mg chol, 363 mg sodium, 804 mg potassium. % RDI: 10% calcium, 29% iron, 10% vit A, 32% vit C, 88% folate.

LEMON-BASIL VINAIGRETTE

½ tsp	grated lemon zest
3 tbsp	lemon juice
1 tbsp	chopped fresh basil
2 tsp	Dijon mustard
¼ tsp	each salt and pepper
¼ cup	extra-virgin olive oil

SALAD

450 g	boneless skinless chicken breasts (about 2)
2 tsp	olive oil
1 tsp	each chopped fresh thyme, fresh tarragon and fresh basil
pinch	each salt and pepper
1½ cup	frozen shelled edamame
1	pkg (142 g) arugula
1 cup	blueberries
⅓ cup	toasted unsalted pumpkin seeds

TIP FROM THE TEST KITCHEN
Flattening the chicken breasts ensures they cook quickly and evenly on the grill.

Panzanella
WITH ASPARAGUS AND EGGS

HANDS-ON TIME	TOTAL TIME	MAKES
15 MINUTES	15 MINUTES	4 SERVINGS

DIJON DRESSING

2 tbsp	extra-virgin olive oil
1 tbsp	red wine vinegar
1 tsp	Dijon mustard
¼ tsp	each salt and pepper

PANZANELLA

4	eggs (shell-on)
pinch	each salt and pepper
2	slices (½-inch thick) sourdough bread
1 tsp	extra-virgin olive oil
1	bunch asparagus (about 450 g), trimmed
1	clove garlic, halved lengthwise
1	avocado, peeled, pitted and sliced
1 cup	halved cherry tomatoes
½ cup	thinly sliced red onion
⅓ cup	torn fresh basil

DIJON DRESSING In small bowl, whisk together oil, vinegar, mustard, salt and pepper. Set aside.

PANZANELLA In saucepan, add eggs and enough water to cover by at least 1 inch; bring to boil. Reduce heat; boil gently for 4 minutes. Remove from heat and let stand for 4 minutes. Drain and run eggs under cold water for 2 minutes; drain. *(Make-ahead: Refrigerate for up to 2 days.)* Peel eggs and halve lengthwise; sprinkle with salt and pepper. Set aside.

Brush both sides of bread with oil. Place bread and asparagus on greased grill over medium-high heat; close lid and grill, turning once, until asparagus is tender and slightly grill-marked and bread is grill-marked, about 7 minutes. Rub both sides of bread with cut sides of garlic; discard garlic. Let cool slightly; cube bread and halve asparagus crosswise.

In large bowl, gently toss together bread, asparagus, avocado, tomatoes, red onion and basil.

Toss bread mixture with dressing to coat. Top with eggs.

NUTRITIONAL INFORMATION, PER SERVING: about 330 cal, 13 g pro, 20 g total fat (4 g sat. fat), 27 g carb (6 g dietary fibre, 4 g sugar), 216 mg chol, 443 mg sodium, 556 mg potassium. % RDI: 7% calcium, 21% iron, 20% vit A, 25% vit C, 88% folate.

Turnip & Kohlrabi Slaw

HANDS-ON TIME	TOTAL TIME	MAKES
15 MINUTES	1¼ HOURS	4 TO 6 SERVINGS

SESAME DRESSING In large bowl, whisk together soy sauce, vinegar, sesame seeds, mustard, sesame oil, garlic and salt. Set aside.

SALAD In saucepan of boiling water, cook edamame for 2 minutes. Drain and rinse under cold water until cool; drain well.

Add edamame, turnip, kohlrabi, carrot and green onions to dressing; toss to coat. Refrigerate for 1 hour before serving.

NUTRITIONAL INFORMATION, PER EACH OF 6 SERVINGS: about 67 cal, 3 g pro, 3 g total fat (trace sat. fat), 8 g carb (3 g dietary fibre, 4 g sugar), 0 mg chol, 265 mg sodium, 287 mg potassium. % RDI: 3% calcium, 6% iron, 21% vit A, 35% vit C, 28% folate.

SESAME DRESSING

4 tsp	sodium-reduced soy sauce
1 tbsp	seasoned rice vinegar
1 tbsp	sesame seeds, toasted
2 tsp	Dijon mustard
1 tsp	sesame oil
1	small clove garlic, finely grated or pressed
pinch	salt

SALAD

1 cup	frozen shelled edamame
2 cups	julienned peeled turnip
1 cup	julienned peeled kohlrabi
1	carrot, julienned
2	green onions, thinly sliced

TIP FROM THE TEST KITCHEN
Try using other julienned root vegetables, such as rutabaga, celery root or carrots, instead of turnip in this slaw.

Bok Choy & Fennel Slaw

HANDS-ON TIME	TOTAL TIME	MAKES
20 MINUTES	4¼ HOURS	6 TO 8 SERVINGS

3 tbsp	lemon juice
2 tbsp	seasoned rice vinegar
1	small garlic clove, minced
¼ tsp	each salt and pepper
pinch	hot pepper flakes (optional)
¼ cup	extra-virgin olive oil
4	heads bok choy (about 350 g total), thinly sliced
1	bulb fennel, trimmed, cored and thinly sliced
1	carrot, julienned

In large bowl, whisk together lemon juice, vinegar, garlic, salt, pepper and hot pepper flakes (if using). Slowly whisk in oil.

Add bok choy, fennel and carrot; toss to combine. Cover and refrigerate for 4 hours. *(Make-ahead: Refrigerate for up to 24 hours.)*

NUTRITIONAL INFORMATION, PER EACH OF 8 SERVINGS: about 86 cal, 1 g pro, 7 g total fat (1 g sat. fat), 6 g carb (2 g dietary fibre, 4 g sugar), 0 mg chol, 256 mg sodium, 269 mg potassium. % RDI: 6% calcium, 5% iron, 35% vit A, 42% vit C, 18% folate.

TIP FROM THE TEST KITCHEN
You can eat this salad right away, but it tastes even better after it has chilled for a while.

Quïnoa Tabbouleh

HANDS-ON TIME	TOTAL TIME	MAKES
15 MINUTES	35 MINUTES	6 SERVINGS

Rinse quinoa under cold running water. In saucepan, bring 1½ cups water to boil; add quinoa and return to boil. Reduce heat, cover and simmer until no liquid remains, about 18 minutes.

Remove from heat; fluff with fork. Transfer to bowl; let cool. Add parsley, cucumber, green onions, mint and tomato.

Whisk together lemon juice, oil, salt and pepper; pour over quinoa mixture and toss to coat. Serve at room temperature, or cover and refrigerate for 1 hour.

NUTRITIONAL INFORMATION, PER SERVING: about 135 cal, 4 g pro, 6 g total fat (1 g sat. fat), 18 g carb (3 g dietary fibre, 1 g sugar), 0 mg chol, 112 mg sodium, 335 mg potassium. % RDI: 4% calcium, 24% iron, 13% vit A, 33% vit C, 18% folate.

¾ cup	quinoa
1 cup	chopped fresh flat-leaf parsley
1 cup	chopped English cucumber
½ cup	chopped green onion
¼ cup	chopped fresh mint
1	tomato, seeded and chopped
3 tbsp	lemon juice
2 tbsp	extra-virgin olive oil
¼ tsp	salt
¼ tsp	pepper

TIP FROM THE TEST KITCHEN
Tabbouleh and many other grain salads keep and travel well, making them good options for school lunches, potlucks and picnics.

Crunchy Curry Rice & Squash

HANDS-ON TIME 20 MINUTES	TOTAL TIME 45 MINUTES	MAKES 4 SERVINGS

4 cups	cubed (½ inch) seeded peeled butternut, turban, acorn or kabocha squash
1 tbsp	olive oil
¼ tsp	each salt and pepper
¼ tsp	ground cumin
1	onion, chopped
2	cloves garlic, chopped
1 cup	basmati rice
1	cinnamon stick
2 tsp	curry powder
2 cups	sodium-reduced chicken broth
⅓ cup	chopped fresh cilantro
¼ cup	roasted almonds, chopped
2 tsp	lemon juice
¼ cup	fresh pomegranate seeds

On greased rimmed baking sheet, toss together squash, half each of the oil, salt and pepper, and the cumin. Bake in 425°F oven, turning once, until tender and golden, about 20 minutes.

Meanwhile, in saucepan, heat remaining oil over medium heat; cook onion, garlic and remaining salt and pepper, stirring often, until onion is translucent, about 3 minutes.

Add rice, cinnamon stick and curry powder; stir to coat. Add broth and bring to boil. Reduce heat, cover and simmer until rice is tender and no liquid remains, about 12 minutes. Let stand, covered, for 5 minutes; fluff with fork. Discard cinnamon stick. Stir in squash, cilantro, almonds and lemon juice. Top with pomegranate seeds.

NUTRITIONAL INFORMATION, PER SERVING: about 353 cal, 9 g pro, 10 g total fat (1 g sat. fat), 61 g carb (5 g dietary fibre, 7 g sugar), 0 mg chol, 450 mg sodium, 659 mg potassium. % RDI: 12% calcium, 15% iron, 175% vit A, 45% vit C, 20% folate.

TIP FROM THE TEST KITCHEN
If you can't find a fresh pomegranate, add the same amount of golden raisins, dried currants or chopped dried apricots instead.

Smoky Lentil Patties
WITH CUCUMBER RADISH SLAW

HANDS-ON TIME	TOTAL TIME	MAKES
25 MINUTES	25 MINUTES	4 SERVINGS

In bowl, whisk together 2 tbsp each of the oil and lemon juice, ¼ tsp of the salt and a pinch of the pepper. Toss in cucumber, radishes, red onion and half of the mint. Let stand for 10 minutes.

Meanwhile, in separate bowl, combine lentils, bread crumbs, egg, green onions, garlic, paprika and ¼ tsp each of the salt, pepper and cumin. Shape by about 2 tbsp into twelve ½-inch thick patties.

In large skillet, heat remaining 3 tbsp oil over medium heat. Cook patties, working in batches and turning once, until crispy and golden, about 10 minutes. Remove from skillet and keep warm.

Meanwhile, in large bowl, stir together lemon zest and yogurt with remaining mint, lemon juice, salt, pepper and cumin.

Serve patties with yogurt dip and cucumber slaw.

NUTRITIONAL INFORMATION, PER SERVING: about 408 cal, 17 g pro, 21 g total fat (4 g sat. fat), 42 g carb (7 g dietary fibre, 8 g sugar), 51 mg chol, 590 mg sodium, 862 mg potassium. % RDI: 17% calcium, 46% iron, 13% vit A, 27% vit C, 110% folate.

5 tbsp	olive oil
½ tsp	lemon zest
3 tbsp	lemon juice
¾ tsp	salt
½ tsp	pepper
1	English cucumber, halved lengthwise and thinly sliced crosswise
16	radishes, thinly sliced
⅔ cup	red onion, thinly sliced
½ cup	chopped fresh mint
2 cups	cooked red lentils, cooled
½ cup	dried bread crumbs
1	egg, lightly beaten
2	green onions, thinly sliced
1	clove garlic, minced
1 tsp	smoked paprika
½ tsp	ground cumin
1 cup	2% Balkan-style plain yogurt

TIP FROM THE TEST KITCHEN
Red lentils break down as they cook, making them perfect for these patties. If you use another variety of lentil, be sure to mash them with the back of a fork before mixing with the other ingredients.

Edamame Guacamole

p.94

HANDS-ON TIME	TOTAL TIME	MAKES
10 MINUTES	10 MINUTES	1½ CUPS

1 cup	frozen shelled edamame
1	avocado, peeled, pitted and chopped
1	green onion, sliced
1 tbsp	lime juice
1	small clove garlic, minced
½ tsp	salt
¼ tsp	pepper
1 tbsp	chopped fresh cilantro

In saucepan of boiling salted water, cook edamame for 1 minute. Drain and let cool to room temperature.

In food processor, purée together edamame, avocado, green onion, lime juice, garlic, salt, pepper and 1 tbsp water until smooth. Stir in cilantro.

NUTRITIONAL INFORMATION, PER 1 TBSP: about 20 cal, 1 g pro, 2 g total fat, 1 g carb (1 g dietary fibre), 0 mg chol, 61 mg sodium, 66 mg potassium. % RDI: 0% calcium, 1% iron, 0% vit A, 2% vit C, 10% folate.

Curried Lentil Dip

HANDS-ON TIME	TOTAL TIME	MAKES
15 MINUTES	1 HOUR	2½ CUPS

2 tbsp	vegetable oil
1	onion, diced
2	cloves garlic, minced
1 tbsp	minced fresh ginger
½ tsp	each garam masala and salt
¼ tsp	each ground cumin, turmeric and pepper
1 cup	dried red lentils

In saucepan, heat oil over medium heat; cook onion, garlic, ginger, garam masala, salt, cumin, turmeric and pepper, stirring occasionally, until onion is softened, about 4 minutes. Stir in lentils; cook, stirring, for 30 seconds.

Stir in 2 cups water; bring to boil. Reduce heat, cover and simmer until lentils are tender and almost no liquid remains, about 15 minutes. Let cool for 10 minutes.

Transfer mixture to food processor; purée, scraping down side of bowl occasionally, until smooth. Let cool. *(Make-ahead: Refrigerate in airtight container for up to 4 days.)*

NUTRITIONAL INFORMATION, PER 1 TBSP: about 24 cal, 1 g pro, 1 g total fat (trace sat. fat), 3 g carb (1 g dietary fibre, trace sugar), 0 mg chol, 29 mg sodium, 58 mg potassium. % RDI: 0% calcium, 4% iron, 0% vit A, 0% vit C, 12% folate.

Sautéed Spinach & Mushrooms

HANDS-ON TIME	TOTAL TIME	MAKES
20 MINUTES	20 MINUTES	6 SERVINGS

In large saucepan of boiling water, working in batches, blanch spinach for 30 seconds. Using slotted spoon, transfer to bowl of ice water to chill. Drain well; squeeze out excess water. Coarsely chop; set aside. *(Make-ahead: Refrigerate in airtight container for up to 24 hours.)*

In large skillet, heat oil over medium-high heat; cook garlic until golden and fragrant, about 1 minute.

Stir in mushrooms; cook, stirring often, until tender and light golden, about 7 minutes.

Stir in spinach, lemon juice, salt and pepper; cook, stirring, for 1 minute.

2	bags (each 225 g) baby spinach
2 tbsp	olive oil
3	cloves garlic, smashed
450 g	oyster mushrooms, trimmed and torn
1 tsp	lemon juice
¼ tsp	each salt and pepper

NUTRITIONAL INFORMATION, PER SERVING: about 85 cal, 5 g pro, 5 g total fat (1 g sat. fat), 8 g carb (4 g dietary fibre, 1 g sugar), 0 mg chol, 160 mg sodium, 659 mg potassium. % RDI: 9% calcium, 26% iron, 76% vit A, 13% vit C, 54% folate.

TIP FROM THE TEST KITCHEN
Leave the garlic cloves in if you're serving garlic lovers; if not, you can remove them just before serving.

Rainbow Root Fries
WITH CHIVE MAYO

HANDS-ON TIME	TOTAL TIME	MAKES
20 MINUTES	1 HOUR	4 TO 6 SERVINGS

ROOT FRIES

1	sweet potato
1	small celery root
1	small rutabaga
1	red beet
2 tbsp	olive oil
1 tsp	each garlic powder and dried rosemary
½ tsp	pepper
¼ tsp	salt
1 tbsp	chopped fresh parsley

CHIVE MAYO

⅓ cup	mayonnaise
1 tbsp	chopped fresh chives
1	small clove garlic, finely grated or pressed
1 tsp	grainy mustard
1 tsp	lemon juice

ROOT FRIES Peel and cut sweet potato, celery root and rutabaga lengthwise into scant ½-inch thick sticks; cut in half crosswise. Transfer each to separate bowl. Set aside.

Peel and cut beet into scant ½-inch thick sticks. Transfer to separate bowl.

Drizzle sweet potato, celery root, rutabaga and beet with oil. Sprinkle with garlic powder, rosemary, salt and pepper; toss each to coat.

Arrange sweet potato, celery root, rutabaga and beet in single layer on parchment paper–lined rimmed baking sheets. Bake in top and bottom thirds of 425°F oven, turning fries once and switching and rotating pans halfway through, until tender and golden, 40 to 45 minutes. Sprinkle with parsley.

CHIVE MAYO While fries are baking, in small bowl, whisk together mayonnaise, chives, garlic, mustard and lemon juice. *(Make-ahead: Refrigerate in airtight container for up to 2 days.)* Serve with fries.

NUTRITIONAL INFORMATION, PER EACH OF 6 SERVINGS: about 245 cal, 4 g pro, 15 g total fat (2 g sat. fat), 27 g carb (5 g dietary fibre, 14 g sugar), 5 mg chol, 292 mg sodium, 776 mg potassium. % RDI: 8% calcium, 12% iron, 91% vit A, 50% vit C, 29% folate.

TIP FROM THE TEST KITCHEN
Keep the beets separated until they're cooked; otherwise they'll stain the other vegetables.

Southwestern Cauliflower Cakes

HANDS-ON TIME	TOTAL TIME	MAKES
30 MINUTES	30 MINUTES	12 CAKES

In covered steamer basket set over saucepan of boiling water, steam cauliflower until tender, about 5 minutes. Transfer to large bowl. Using potato masher, mash until cauliflower resembles coarse crumbs. Set aside.

In separate bowl, whisk together eggs, mustard, chili powder, garlic, salt and pepper. Add cauliflower, bread crumbs, corn and half of the chives; stir until well combined. Shape by 2 tbsp into twelve 1½-inch wide patties.

In large nonstick skillet, heat oil over medium heat. Working in batches, cook patties, flattening with spatula and turning once, until browned and heated through, about 6 minutes.

Top with sour cream and remaining chives.

NUTRITIONAL INFORMATION, PER CAKE: about 83 cal, 3 g pro, 5 g total fat (1 g sat. fat), 8 g carb (1 g dietary fibre, 1 g sugar), 133 mg chol, 136 mg sodium, 107 mg potassium. % RDI: 3% calcium, 5% iron, 3% vit A, 25% vit C, 14% folate.

4 cups	bite-size cauliflower florets (about half a head)
2	eggs
1 tbsp	grainy mustard
1 tsp	chili powder
1	clove garlic, pressed or grated
¼ tsp	each salt and pepper
¾ cup	dried bread crumbs
½ cup	frozen corn kernels
2 tbsp	chopped fresh chives
2 tbsp	olive oil
⅓ cup	light sour cream

Cauliflower Corn Chowder

HANDS-ON TIME 30 MINUTES	TOTAL TIME 30 MINUTES	MAKES 6 SERVINGS

2 tbsp	olive oil
1	onion, diced
4	cloves garlic, minced
1 tbsp	chopped fresh thyme
3	corn cobs, husked and kernels removed
1	small head cauliflower, cut in bite-size florets (about 6 cups)
3 cups	sodium-reduced vegetable broth
¼ tsp	each salt and pepper
1½ cups	milk
3 tbsp	all-purpose flour
1	sweet red pepper, diced
2 tbsp	lemon juice

In Dutch oven or large heavy-bottomed saucepan, heat oil over medium-high heat; sauté onion, garlic and 2 tsp of the thyme until onion is softened, about 3 minutes. Stir in corn kernels, cauliflower, broth, salt, pepper and ½ cup water; bring to boil. Reduce heat, cover and simmer until cauliflower is tender, about 8 minutes.

In blender, working in batches, purée 4 cups of the soup until smooth; return to pot. Whisk milk with flour; stir into soup. Add red pepper; bring to boil. Reduce heat; simmer, uncovered and stirring occasionally, just until red pepper is tender and soup is slightly thickened, about 2 minutes. Stir in lemon juice. Sprinkle with remaining thyme.

NUTRITIONAL INFORMATION, PER SERVING: about 198 cal, 7 g pro, 7 g total fat (1 g sat. fat), 31 g carb (6 g dietary fibre, 9 g sugar), 5 mg chol, 221 mg sodium, 446 mg potassium. % RDI: 10% calcium, 10% iron, 11% vit A, 133% vit C, 38% folate.

VARIATION
Chicken and Cauliflower Corn Chowder
Stir in 2 cups chopped cooked chicken breast along with the red pepper.

TIP FROM THE TEST KITCHEN
When blending hot liquids, remove the blender lid insert to relieve pressure caused by steam; cover the vent hole with a folded kitchen towel.

Chicken, Rice & Thyme Biryani

HANDS-ON TIME	TOTAL TIME	MAKES
20 MINUTES	45 MINUTES	4 SERVINGS

Sprinkle chicken with ¼ tsp salt and the pepper. In Dutch oven or large heavy-bottomed saucepan, heat oil over medium-high heat; cook chicken, turning occasionally, until golden, about 7 minutes. Transfer to plate.

Drain all but 4 tsp fat from pan; cook onions over medium-high heat, stirring, until golden, about 6 minutes. Stir in broth, rice, thyme and remaining salt, scraping up browned bits; bring to boil.

Arrange chicken, skin side up, over rice mixture. Reduce heat, cover and simmer until liquid is absorbed and juices run clear when thickest parts of thighs are pierced, about 15 minutes. Remove from heat; let stand, covered, for 10 minutes before serving.

NUTRITIONAL INFORMATION, PER SERVING: about 468 cal, 26 g pro, 21 g total fat (6 g sat. fat), 42 g carb (2 g dietary fibre, 3 g sugar), 101 mg chol, 681 mg sodium, 370 mg potassium. % RDI: 4% calcium, 12% iron, 5% vit A, 12% vit C, 10% folate.

4	bone-in skin-on chicken thighs (about 400 g)
½ tsp	salt
pinch	pepper
1 tsp	olive oil
2	onions, thinly sliced
2 cups	sodium-reduced chicken broth
1 cup	basmati rice, rinsed
1 tbsp	finely chopped fresh thyme

SERVE WITH
Chunky Mango Raita

In small dry skillet over medium heat, toast ½ tsp cumin seeds until beginning to darken, about 1 minute; let cool. With side of knife, coarsely crush seeds; set aside.

In small bowl, stir together 2 cups Balkan-style plain yogurt, 8 chopped pitted dates, 1 diced peeled mango, 4 tsp lime juice, 1 tbsp chopped fresh mint and ¼ tsp salt. *(Make-ahead: Cover and refrigerate for up to 24 hours.)* Sprinkle with cumin seeds.

Jerk Chicken One-Pan Dinner

p.7

HANDS-ON TIME 10 MINUTES	TOTAL TIME 50 MINUTES	MAKES 4 SERVINGS

2 tsp	dried thyme
1 tsp	garlic powder
¾ tsp	salt
½ tsp	each ground allspice, ground coriander and ground ginger
¼ tsp	pepper
pinch	cayenne pepper
900 g	skin-on chicken drumsticks (about 8 drumsticks)
300 g	white or yellow-fleshed potato (about 1), cut in wedges
300 g	sweet potato (about 1), cut in wedges
1	sweet red pepper, cut in 1-inch thick slices
1	small onion, cut in wedges

In small bowl, stir together thyme, garlic powder, salt, allspice, coriander, ginger, pepper and cayenne pepper.

In plastic bag, add chicken and 4 tsp of the thyme mixture. Holding bag closed, shake to coat chicken.

In lightly greased large roasting pan, toss together potato, sweet potato, red pepper, onion and remaining thyme mixture; arrange vegetables in single layer. Add chicken.

Bake in 425°F oven until juices run clear when thickest parts of chicken are pierced and potatoes are softened, about 40 minutes. Broil until chicken and vegetables are golden, about 3 minutes.

NUTRITIONAL INFORMATION, PER SERVING: about 388 cal, 28 g pro, 16 g total fat (4 g sat. fat), 34 g carb (5 g dietary fibre, 8 g sugar), 102 mg chol, 559 mg sodium, 888 mg potassium. % RDI: 6% calcium, 26% iron, 133% vit A, 150% vit C, 16% folate.

SERVE WITH
Pineapple Salad

In large bowl, whisk together 4 tsp vegetable oil, 1½ tsp lime juice, ½ tsp liquid honey and pinch each salt and pepper. Add 6 cups mixed baby greens, 1 cup chopped cored peeled pineapple and ¼ cup thinly sliced red onion; toss to coat.

Chicken & Kale Stew
WITH CHILI YOGURT

p.5

HANDS-ON TIME	TOTAL TIME	MAKES
30 MINUTES	30 MINUTES	6 SERVINGS

CHICKEN AND KALE STEW In Dutch oven or large heavy-bottomed saucepan, heat oil over medium-high heat; cook squash and onion, stirring occasionally, until onion is beginning to soften, about 4 minutes. Add garlic, chili pepper and ginger; cook, stirring, for 1 minute.

Stir in broth, sage, thyme, pepper and salt; bring to boil. Reduce heat and simmer, stirring occasionally, for 5 minutes. Add chicken; simmer, stirring occasionally, for 5 minutes.

Using slotted spoon, transfer chili pepper to cutting board; mince chili pepper. Reserve for Chili Yogurt.

Add kale and corn to pan; cook, stirring occasionally, until kale is wilted and chicken is no longer pink inside, about 2 minutes. Stir in lemon juice.

Whisk cornstarch with 2 tbsp water; stir into pan. Bring to boil; cook, stirring, until thickened, about 1 minute. Ladle stew into serving bowls.

CHILI YOGURT In small bowl, stir together yogurt, chives, lemon juice and reserved chili pepper; dollop over stew. Sprinkle with sunflower seeds.

NUTRITIONAL INFORMATION, PER SERVING: about 195 cal, 23 g pro, 4 g total fat (1 g sat. fat), 18 g carb (3 g dietary fibre, 4 g sugar), 44 mg chol, 532 mg sodium, 588 mg potassium. % RDI: 8% calcium, 11% iron, 94% vit A, 50% vit C, 15% folate.

CHICKEN AND KALE STEW

1 tsp	olive oil
2½ cups	cubed seeded peeled butternut squash
1	onion, thinly sliced
2	cloves garlic, pressed or grated
1	small finger chili pepper (red or yellow), halved lengthwise and seeded
1 tbsp	minced peeled fresh ginger
1	pkg (900 mL) sodium-reduced chicken broth
½ tsp	each dried sage and dried thyme
½ tsp	pepper
¼ tsp	salt
450 g	boneless skinless chicken breasts, cubed
4 cups	chopped stemmed kale
½ cup	frozen corn kernels
1 tsp	lemon juice
2 tbsp	cornstarch

CHILI YOGURT

⅓ cup	2% plain Greek yogurt
1 tbsp	chopped fresh chives
½ tsp	lemon juice
2 tbsp	sunflower seeds, toasted

Quick Chicken & White Bean Stew

HANDS-ON TIME	TOTAL TIME	MAKES
25 MINUTES	30 MINUTES	4 SERVINGS

2	strips bacon, thinly sliced
450 g	boneless skinless chicken thighs, quartered
2 tsp	vegetable oil
1	onion, sliced
6	cloves garlic, sliced
1 tbsp	chopped fresh thyme
1	pkg (227 g) cremini or button mushrooms, sliced
1	can (540 mL) navy beans, drained and rinsed
2 cups	bottled strained tomatoes (passata)
pinch	each salt and pepper
2	green onions, sliced
2 tbsp	chopped fresh parsley
1 tsp	red wine vinegar

In Dutch oven or large heavy-bottomed saucepan, cook bacon over medium heat, stirring, until fat begins to render, about 2 minutes.

Add chicken; cook, stirring, until browned, about 4 minutes. Using slotted spoon, transfer mixture to plate; set aside.

In same pan, heat oil over medium heat; cook onion, stirring, until softened, about 3 minutes. Add garlic and thyme; cook, stirring, until fragrant, about 1 minute. Add mushrooms and 2 tbsp water; cook, stirring occasionally and scraping up browned bits, until mushrooms are tender and no liquid remains, 4 to 5 minutes.

Return chicken mixture and any juices to pan. Stir in beans, strained tomatoes, salt, pepper and ½ cup water; bring to boil. Reduce heat, cover and simmer until stew is slightly thickened and chicken is no longer pink inside, about 8 minutes. Remove from heat; stir in green onions, parsley and vinegar.

NUTRITIONAL INFORMATION, PER SERVING: about 449 cal, 35 g pro, 14 g total fat (5 g sat. fat), 45 g carb (10 g dietary fibre, 8 g sugar), 101 mg chol, 418 mg sodium, 1,204 mg potassium. % RDI: 11% calcium, 48% iron, 4% vit A, 18% vit C, 40% folate.

TIP FROM THE TEST KITCHEN
Passata is a purée of lightly cooked, strained tomatoes. Look for bottles of passata near the canned tomatoes in the grocery store.

30-Minute Turkey Chili

HANDS-ON TIME	TOTAL TIME	MAKES
30 MINUTES	30 MINUTES	4 SERVINGS

In Dutch oven or large heavy-bottomed saucepan, heat oil over medium-high heat; cook onion and garlic, stirring, until just beginning to soften, about 3 minutes. Stir in turkey, carrot, celery, mushrooms and red pepper; cook, breaking up turkey with spoon, until turkey is no longer pink, about 5 minutes. Stir in chili powder, cumin, coriander, oregano and salt; cook, stirring, for 2 minutes.

Stir in tomatoes and tomato paste; bring to boil. Reduce heat and simmer, stirring occasionally, for 10 minutes. Add chickpeas and spinach; cook, stirring occasionally, for 5 minutes.

NUTRITIONAL INFORMATION, PER SERVING: about 401 cal, 30 g pro, 16 g total fat (3 g sat. fat), 38 g carb (11 g dietary fibre, 13 g sugar), 89 mg chol, 600 mg sodium, 1,290 mg potassium. % RDI: 18% calcium, 51% iron, 78% vit A, 105% vit C, 51% folate.

1 tbsp	vegetable oil
1	onion, diced
3	cloves garlic, minced
450 g	extra-lean ground turkey
1	carrot, diced
1	rib celery, diced
1	pkg (227 g) cremini or button mushrooms, diced
half	sweet red pepper, diced
4 tsp	chili powder
1 tsp	each ground cumin and ground coriander
½ tsp	dried oregano
1	can (796 mL) whole tomatoes, crushed by hand
2 tbsp	tomato paste
1	can (540 mL) chickpeas, drained and rinsed
4 cups	lightly packed baby spinach

SERVE WITH
Cornmeal Buttermilk Drop Biscuits

In bowl, whisk together 1½ cups all-purpose flour, ½ cup cornmeal, 1 tbsp granulated sugar, 2 tsp baking powder, ½ tsp baking soda and a pinch salt. Cut in ½ cup cold butter, cubed. With fork, stir in ¾ cup buttermilk until mixture forms soft dough. Drop 12 equal portions onto parchment paper–lined baking sheet. Bake in 400°F (200°C) oven until bottoms are golden and biscuits are puffed and flaky, 12 to 15 minutes.

One-Pot Pasta
WITH SHRIMP, TOMATOES & FETA

HANDS-ON TIME	TOTAL TIME	MAKES
20 MINUTES	20 MINUTES	4 TO 6 SERVINGS

340 g	spaghetti
2 tbsp	olive oil
4	cloves garlic, sliced
1 tsp	dried oregano
¼ tsp	hot pepper flakes
450 g	jumbo shrimp (21 to 25 count), peeled and deveined
half	red onion, sliced
3 cups	halved cherry tomatoes (about 475 g)
¼ cup	pitted Kalamata olives, chopped
⅓ cup	chopped fresh parsley
¼ cup	crumbled feta cheese

In large saucepan of boiling salted water, cook pasta according to package instructions. Reserving ½ cup of the cooking liquid, drain. Set aside.

In same pan, heat oil over medium heat; cook garlic, oregano and hot pepper flakes, stirring, until fragrant, about 30 seconds. Add shrimp and onion; cook, stirring, until shrimp are beginning to turn pink, about 1 minute. Add tomatoes and olives; cook, stirring occasionally, until shrimp are pink and opaque throughout and tomatoes are beginning to soften, about 2 minutes.

Stir in pasta, parsley and reserved cooking liquid; cook for 1 minute. Top with feta.

NUTRITIONAL INFORMATION, PER EACH OF 6 SERVINGS: about 374 cal, 22 g pro, 10 g total fat (2 g sat. fat), 50 g carb (3 g dietary fibre, 4 g sugar), 91 mg chol, 490 mg sodium, 424 mg potassium. % RDI: 9% calcium, 27% iron, 13% vit A, 27% vit C, 69% folate.

Pork in Mushroom Gravy
WITH EGG NOODLES

HANDS-ON TIME	TOTAL TIME	MAKES
30 MINUTES	30 MINUTES	4 SERVINGS

Sprinkle pork with pepper and salt. In nonstick skillet, heat half of the oil over medium-high heat; cook pork, turning once, until browned, about 5 minutes. Transfer to plate; keep warm.

In same pan, heat remaining oil over medium heat; cook mushrooms, garlic and thyme, stirring occasionally, until almost no liquid remains, about 6 minutes. Scrape into bowl; keep warm.

Whisk together broth, cornstarch and ¾ cup water; stir into pan. Bring to simmer; cook, scraping up browned bits, until thickened, about 5 minutes.

Return pork and any juices and the mushroom mixture to pan; cook, stirring, until sauce is glossy and thickened, about 3 minutes. Stir in sour cream, mustard and vinegar; cook until juices run clear when pork is pierced and just a hint of pink remains inside, about 2 minutes. Stir in parsley.

Meanwhile, in large saucepan of boiling lightly salted water, cook noodles according to package instructions, adding peas in last 3 minutes of cook time. Drain. Serve pork mixture over noodles and peas.

NUTRITIONAL INFORMATION, PER SERVING: about 345 cal, 33 g pro, 8 g total fat (2 g sat. fat), 35 g carb (5 g dietary fibre, 4 g sugar), 91 mg chol, 436 mg sodium, 1,011 mg potassium. % RDI: 6% calcium, 29% iron, 7% vit A, 10% vit C, 57% folate.

450 g	pork tenderloin, trimmed and cut in 1-inch thick rounds
¼ tsp	pepper
pinch	salt
1 tbsp	olive oil
2	pkg (each 227 g) cremini mushrooms, sliced
3	cloves garlic, minced
2 tsp	chopped fresh thyme
¾ cup	sodium-reduced chicken broth
2 tsp	cornstarch
2 tbsp	light sour cream
2 tsp	Dijon mustard
1 tsp	balsamic vinegar
2 tbsp	chopped fresh parsley
140 g	egg noodles
½ cup	frozen peas

TIP FROM THE TEST KITCHEN
Cremini, button and portobello mushrooms are all the same species at different stages of maturity. They're easily substituted for each other in this and many other dishes.

Lemony Angel Hair Pasta
WITH PAN-FRIED CHICKEN

HANDS-ON TIME	TOTAL TIME	MAKES
15 MINUTES	20 MINUTES	4 SERVINGS

450 g	chicken cutlets
pinch	each salt and pepper
4 tsp	olive oil
2 tbsp	capers, rinsed, drained and chopped
1 cup	cherry tomatoes, halved
280 g	angel hair pasta
2 tsp	grated lemon zest
3 tbsp	lemon juice

Sprinkle chicken with salt and pepper. In skillet, heat 2 tsp of the oil over medium-high heat; cook chicken, turning once, until no longer pink inside, about 6 minutes. Remove from pan and keep warm.

In same pan, heat remaining oil over medium-high heat; add capers and warm through, about 30 seconds. Add tomatoes and pinch each salt and pepper; cook until tomatoes start to soften, about 2 minutes.

Meanwhile, in large saucepan of boiling salted water, cook pasta according to package instructions. Reserving ½ cup of the cooking liquid, drain.

Stir pasta and reserved cooking liquid into skillet; remove from heat. Stir in lemon zest and lemon juice. Serve with chicken.

NUTRITIONAL INFORMATION, PER SERVING: about 440 cal, 35 g pro, 8 g total fat (1 g sat. fat), 56 g carb (4 g dietary fibre, 2 g sugar), 66 mg chol, 467 mg sodium, 489 mg potassium. % RDI: 2% calcium, 24% iron, 4% vit A, 20% vit C, 70% folate.

Penne With Shrimp
IN TOMATO & MINT SAUCE

HANDS-ON TIME	TOTAL TIME	MAKES
30 MINUTES	30 MINUTES	4 TO 6 SERVINGS

Score an X in bottom of each tomato. In saucepan of boiling water, blanch tomatoes until skins start to loosen, about 15 seconds; drain and let cool. Peel off skins. Cut each in half crosswise; seed and slice into thin strips.

In large saucepan of boiling salted water, cook pasta according to package instructions. Reserving some of the cooking liquid, drain.

Meanwhile, in skillet, heat oil over medium-high heat; sauté garlic, fennel seeds and hot pepper flakes until fragrant, about 30 seconds. Stir in shrimp; sauté until pink and opaque throughout, 2 to 3 minutes. Add parsley and salt; sauté until parsley begins to wilt, about 30 seconds.

Stir in tomatoes; sauté just until softened, about 2 minutes. Add mint, capers and lemon juice; sauté for 30 seconds. Stir in some of the reserved cooking liquid to thin out sauce as needed. Serve over pasta.

675 g	tomatoes
450 g	penne
3 tbsp	olive oil
4	cloves garlic, minced
½ tsp	fennel seeds
¼ tsp	hot pepper flakes
450 g	medium shrimp (51 to 60 count), peeled and deveined
¼ cup	chopped fresh parsley
½ tsp	salt
1 cup	loosely packed fresh mint leaves, chopped
2 tbsp	drained capers
4 tsp	lemon juice

NUTRITIONAL INFORMATION, PER EACH OF 6 SERVINGS: about 434 cal, 26 g pro, 10 g total fat (1 g sat. fat), 60 g carb (5 g dietary fibre, 2 g sugar), 115 mg chol, 594 mg sodium, 325 mg potassium. % RDI: 7% calcium, 41% iron, 11% vit A, 15% vit C, 78% folate.

VARIATION
Penne With Calamari in Tomato and Mint Sauce
Replace shrimp with cleaned squid. Cut tentacles into 2 pieces; slice tubes into thin rings. Sauté until opaque, about 2 minutes. Continue with recipe.

Singapore Noodles

HANDS-ON TIME 30 MINUTES	TOTAL TIME 50 MINUTES	MAKES 4 TO 6 SERVINGS

225 g	pork tenderloin, trimmed and thinly sliced
2 tbsp	sodium-reduced soy sauce
1 tsp	sesame oil
½ tsp	salt
¼ tsp	pepper
280 g	dried rice vermicelli (about ⅟₃₂-inch wide)
	boiling water
4 tsp	vegetable oil
2	eggs, lightly beaten
225 g	jumbo shrimp (21 to 25 count), peeled and deveined
1	small onion, thinly sliced
half	sweet red pepper, thinly sliced
2	cloves garlic, minced
2	green onions, cut in 1½-inch lengths
2 tsp	curry powder
1 tsp	turmeric
1 tsp	granulated sugar
2 cups	bean sprouts

In bowl, stir together pork, 2 tsp of the soy sauce, the sesame oil, pinch of the salt, and the pepper. Cover and refrigerate for 30 minutes. *(Make-ahead: Refrigerate for up to 24 hours.)*

Meanwhile, in large bowl, add vermicelli and enough boiling water to cover; soak according to package instructions. Drain and rinse under cold water; drain well.

In wok or large nonstick skillet, heat 1 tsp of the vegetable oil over medium-high heat; cook eggs, stirring, just until set, about 1 minute. Scrape onto plate. Wipe pan clean. Add 1 tsp of the vegetable oil to pan; sauté shrimp over medium-high heat until pink and opaque throughout, about 2 minutes. Transfer to plate. Add 1 tsp of the vegetable oil to pan; sauté pork mixture over medium-high heat until just a hint of pink remains inside, about 3 minutes. Transfer to plate.

Add remaining vegetable oil to pan; sauté onion, red pepper and garlic over medium-high heat until pepper is tender-crisp, about 2 minutes. Add pork, vermicelli, eggs, shrimp, green onions, curry powder, turmeric, sugar and remaining soy sauce and salt. Cook, stirring and tossing, until well combined and heated through, about 3 minutes. Add bean sprouts; cook, stirring, until softened, about 1 minute.

NUTRITIONAL INFORMATION, PER EACH OF 6 SERVINGS: about 330 cal, 19 g pro, 7 g total fat (1 g sat. fat), 46 g carb (3 g dietary fibre, 4 g sugar), 124 mg chol, 504 mg sodium, 328 mg potassium. % RDI: 4% calcium, 18% iron, 8% vit A, 37% vit C, 18% folate.

VARIATION
Vegetarian Singapore Noodles
Omit shrimp. Substitute 1 pkg (350 g) extra-firm tofu, drained and cut in ½-inch cubes, for the pork; continue with recipe as directed.

Spicy Ginger & Green Onion Noodle Salad
WITH GRILLED CHICKEN

HANDS-ON TIME	TOTAL TIME	MAKES
20 MINUTES	25 MINUTES	4 SERVINGS

Sprinkle chicken with a pinch each of the salt and pepper. Place on greased grill over medium-high heat; close lid and grill, turning once, until no longer pink inside, about 12 minutes. Tent with foil; let stand for 5 minutes before thinly slicing crosswise.

Meanwhile, in large bowl, add vermicelli and enough boiling water to cover; soak according to package instructions. Drain and rinse under cold water; drain well.

Meanwhile, in small saucepan, heat oil over medium heat; cook ginger and garlic, stirring, until fragrant, about 2 minutes. Stir in green onions and remaining salt and pepper; cook until onions are softened, about 2 minutes. Remove from heat; stir in lime juice, soy sauce, honey and chili sauce.

In large bowl, toss ginger mixture with vermicelli, red pepper, carrot and cucumber. Top with chicken.

NUTRITIONAL INFORMATION, PER SERVING: about 478 cal, 29 g pro, 13 g total fat (1 g sat. fat), 60 g carb (4 g dietary fibre, 7 g sugar), 66 mg chol, 446 mg sodium, 648 mg potassium. % RDI: 5% calcium, 12% iron, 51% vit A, 75% vit C, 21% folate.

2	boneless skinless chicken breasts (about 450 g total)
¼ tsp	each salt and pepper
225 g	dried rice vermicelli (about ⅛-inch wide)
3 tbsp	vegetable oil
2 tbsp	minced fresh ginger
4	cloves garlic, minced
8	green onions, thinly sliced
4 tsp	lime juice
4 tsp	sodium-reduced soy sauce
2 tsp	liquid honey
½ tsp	Asian chili sauce (such as sriracha)
1	sweet red pepper, thinly sliced
1	large carrot, julienned
half	cucumber, chopped

TIP FROM THE TEST KITCHEN
Be careful not to soak the rice noodles too long; they can become mushy. You can substitute other Asian noodles, such as bean-thread or soba noodles, cooked according to package instructions.

Turkey & Caramelized Onion Fusilli

HANDS-ON TIME	TOTAL TIME	MAKES
30 MINUTES	30 MINUTES	4 SERVINGS

½ cup	chopped fresh parsley
1 tbsp	capers, drained, rinsed and chopped
1	small clove garlic, pressed or grated
6½ tsp	olive oil
1 tsp	grated lemon zest
1 tsp	lemon juice
375 g	fusilli
2	onions, sliced
1 tsp	white wine vinegar
pinch	each granulated sugar, salt and pepper
2 cups	shredded skinless cooked roast turkey or chicken (white or dark meat)
⅔ cup	sodium-reduced chicken broth

In small bowl, stir together parsley, capers, garlic, 2 tsp of the oil, the lemon zest and lemon juice. Set aside.

In large saucepan of boiling salted water, cook pasta according to package instructions. Reserving ½ cup of the cooking liquid, drain. Set aside.

While pasta is cooking, in large nonstick skillet, heat remaining oil over medium heat; cook onions, stirring occasionally, until softened and golden, 12 to 15 minutes. Add vinegar, sugar, salt and pepper; cook, stirring, for 2 minutes. Add turkey and broth; cook, stirring occasionally, until heated through, about 3 minutes.

Stir in pasta and reserved cooking liquid, tossing to coat. Stir in parsley mixture.

NUTRITIONAL INFORMATION, PER SERVING: about 559 cal, 33 g pro, 13 g total fat (2 g sat. fat), 76 g carb (4 g dietary fibre, 4 g sugar), 48 mg chol, 558 mg sodium, 414 mg potassium. % RDI: 5% calcium, 34% iron, 6% vit A, 23% vit C, 106% folate.

TIP FROM THE TEST KITCHEN
Many pasta recipes call for reserving some of the cooking liquid—the starch in the liquid helps bind the sauce to the pasta. And if a pasta sauce has become too thick, thin it with a little of the cooking liquid.

Chicken & Swiss Chard
WITH SOBA NOODLES

HANDS-ON TIME	TOTAL TIME	MAKES
20 MINUTES	20 MINUTES	4 SERVINGS

In small bowl, whisk together soy sauce, lime juice and sesame oil; set aside. In large nonstick skillet or wok, heat vegetable oil over medium-high heat; cook chicken, ginger and garlic, stirring often, until chicken is light golden, about 3 minutes.

Stir in Swiss chard and yellow pepper; stir-fry until chard starts to wilt, about 2 minutes.

Meanwhile, in large saucepan of boiling water, cook noodles according to package instructions; drain. Add noodles to skillet along with snow peas and soy sauce mixture; stir-fry for 1 minute. Transfer to platter. Sprinkle with sesame seeds.

NUTRITIONAL INFORMATION, PER SERVING: about 310 cal, 24 g pro, 7 g total fat (1 g sat. fat), 42 g carb (5 g dietary fibre, 4 g sugar), 33 mg chol, 417 mg sodium, 819 mg potassium. % RDI: 8% calcium, 29% iron, 47% vit A, 143% vit C, 20% folate.

4 tsp	sodium-reduced soy sauce
1 tbsp	lime juice
2 tsp	sesame oil
2 tsp	vegetable oil
225 g	boneless skinless chicken breast, thinly sliced
1 tbsp	grated fresh ginger
3	cloves garlic, minced
8 cups	chopped stemmed Swiss chard (about 1 bunch)
1	sweet yellow pepper, sliced
170 g	soba noodles
4 cups	trimmed snow peas
2 tsp	sesame seeds, toasted

TIP FROM THE TEST KITCHEN
Toast sesame seeds in a dry skillet over medium-high heat, stirring frequently, until golden, 3 to 5 minutes. Watch them carefully; sesame seeds can go from toasted to burnt very quickly.

Stir-Fried Mongolian Noodles
WITH CHICKEN

HANDS-ON TIME 20 MINUTES	TOTAL TIME 20 MINUTES	MAKES 4 SERVINGS

4 tsp	vegetable oil
2	boneless skinless chicken breasts (about 450 g total), thinly sliced crosswise
2	pkg (each 200 g) udon noodles
4 cups	broccoli florets
1 tbsp	hoisin sauce
1 tbsp	sodium-reduced soy sauce
¼ tsp	pepper
4	cloves garlic, minced
1	red finger chili pepper, thinly sliced

In large wok or nonstick skillet, heat 1 tbsp of the oil over medium-high heat; stir-fry chicken until golden and no longer pink inside, about 5 minutes. Transfer to plate; set aside.

Meanwhile, in large saucepan of boiling water, cook noodles and broccoli until noodles are tender and broccoli is tender-crisp, about 3 minutes; drain well.

In bowl, stir together hoisin sauce, soy sauce, pepper and ⅓ cup water.

In wok, heat remaining oil over medium-high heat; stir-fry garlic and chili pepper until fragrant, about 30 seconds. Add chicken, noodle mixture and hoisin sauce mixture; stir-fry until coated and sauce is slightly thickened, about 2 minutes.

NUTRITIONAL INFORMATION, PER SERVING: about 486 cal, 35 g pro, 8 g total fat (2 g sat. fat), 64 g carb (2 g dietary fibre, 4 g sugar), 65 mg chol, 423 mg sodium, 601 mg potassium. % RDI: 6% calcium, 14% iron, 22% vit A, 73% vit C, 17% folate.

TIP FROM THE TEST KITCHEN
Quick-cooking udon noodles can usually be found in convenient 200 g packages in the Asian section of your grocery store.

Butternut Squash Mac & Cheese

HANDS-ON TIME	TOTAL TIME	MAKES
30 MINUTES	30 MINUTES	4 SERVINGS

In large saucepan of boiling salted water, cook squash until tender and pasta according to package instructions until al dente, about 12 minutes for squash. (The squash may need to cook for a few minutes before pasta is added, depending on pasta cook time listed on package instructions.) Drain; set aside.

Meanwhile, in separate large saucepan, melt butter over medium heat; cook sage and garlic, stirring occasionally, until fragrant, about 1 minute. Whisk in flour; cook, whisking constantly, for 1 minute. Whisk in milk in slow, steady stream; cook, whisking often, until beginning to thicken, 6 to 8 minutes. Stir in pasta and squash; cook until sauce is thickened, about 3 minutes. Stir in Cheddar until melted and smooth, about 1 minute. Remove from heat; stir in green onions, mustard, salt, pepper, nutmeg and cayenne pepper. Serve immediately.

NUTRITIONAL INFORMATION, PER SERVING: about 311 cal, 13 g pro, 8 g total fat (4 g sat. fat), 47 g carb (3 g dietary fibre, 9 g sugar), 22 mg chol, 530 mg sodium, 565 mg potassium. % RDI: 24% calcium, 16% iron, 121% vit A, 27% vit C, 50% folate.

2½ cups	chopped seeded peeled butternut squash (generous ½-inch chunks)
1¼ cups	elbow macaroni
2 tsp	unsalted butter
6	fresh sage leaves, chopped
3	cloves garlic, minced
3 tbsp	all-purpose flour
2 cups	milk
3 tbsp	cold-pack sharp Cheddar cheese product (such as MacLaren's Imperial)
2	green onions, sliced
1 tsp	Dijon mustard
pinch	each salt, pepper, nutmeg and cayenne pepper

TIP FROM THE TEST KITCHEN
Unlike most other winter squashes, butternut squash has a thin skin that's easily removed with a vegetable peeler. For a healthful snack, don't throw away the seeds—toast them as you would pumpkin seeds.

Creamy Pasta Shells
WITH CAULIFLOWER SAUCE

HANDS-ON TIME	TOTAL TIME	MAKES
30 MINUTES	30 MINUTES	4 SERVINGS

6 cups	cauliflower florets (about 500 g)
2	cloves garlic, halved
⅓ cup	grated Parmesan cheese
2 tbsp	whipping cream (35%)
1 tsp	Dijon mustard
¼ tsp	salt
pinch	pepper
375 g	small shell pasta
1 cup	frozen peas
2 tsp	lemon juice
4	strips sodium-reduced bacon, cooked and chopped

In large saucepan of boiling salted water, cook cauliflower and garlic until tender, about 10 minutes. Reserving 1 cup of the cooking liquid, drain. Transfer cauliflower mixture to blender; pulse until coarsely chopped. Add Parmesan, cream, mustard, salt, pepper and reserved cauliflower cooking liquid; purée until smooth.

Meanwhile, in large saucepan of boiling water, cook pasta according to package instructions, adding peas during last 2 minutes. Reserving ½ cup of the cooking liquid, drain. Return to pot; stir in cauliflower mixture, lemon juice, bacon and enough of the reserved pasta cooking liquid to coat.

NUTRITIONAL INFORMATION, PER SERVING: about 501 cal, 23 g pro, 9 g total fat (4 g sat. fat), 82 g carb (8 g dietary fibre, 5 g sugar), 30 mg chol, 405 mg sodium, 440 mg potassium. % RDI: 14% calcium, 32% iron, 10% vit A, 113% vit C, 125% folate.

VARIATION
Baked Creamy Pasta Shells With Cauliflower Sauce
Complete recipe as above. Transfer to lightly greased 12-cup casserole dish. Sprinkle with ½ cup shredded mozzarella cheese. Bake in 425°F oven until mozzarella is melted, 5 to 7 minutes; broil until cheese is bubbly and golden, about 3 minutes.

Zucchini Ribbon & Caper Pasta

p.159

HANDS-ON TIME	TOTAL TIME	MAKES
20 MINUTES	20 MINUTES	4 SERVINGS

In large saucepan of boiling salted water, cook pasta according to package directions. Reserving ⅓ cup of the cooking liquid, drain.

Meanwhile, using vegetable peeler, slice zucchini lengthwise into long ribbons. In large skillet, heat oil over medium heat; cook zucchini, onion and capers, stirring occasionally, until onion is softened, about 5 minutes. Add garlic, lemon zest and hot pepper flakes; cook, stirring, for 1 minute.

Stir in pasta, Parmesan, lemon juice and enough of the reserved pasta cooking liquid to coat; sprinkle with salt and pepper.

NUTRITIONAL INFORMATION, PER SERVING: about 417 cal, 15 g pro, 7 g total fat (2 g sat. fat), 75 g carb (7 g dietary fibre, 6 g sugar), 5 mg chol, 421 mg sodium, 557 mg potassium. % RDI: 11% calcium, 28% iron, 19% vit A, 18% vit C, 94% folate.

340 g	spaghetti
4	zucchini
1 tbsp	olive oil
half	red onion, thinly sliced
1 tbsp	capers, drained and rinsed
1	clove garlic, crushed
2 tsp	grated lemon zest
pinch	hot pepper flakes
¼ cup	grated Parmesan cheese
1 tbsp	lemon juice
pinch	each salt and pepper

Steakhouse Sliders
WITH GRILLED ONIONS

HANDS-ON TIME 25 MINUTES	TOTAL TIME 30 MINUTES	MAKES 12 SLIDERS

HORSERADISH SAUCE

¼ cup	light mayonnaise
1 tbsp	Dijon mustard
1 tbsp	prepared horseradish
pinch	pepper

SLIDERS

1 tsp	vegetable oil
2	cloves garlic, minced
1	pkg (227 g) cremini mushrooms, cut in ¼-inch pieces
1	egg, beaten
2 tbsp	prepared steak sauce (such as HP)
1 tbsp	Dijon mustard
1 tsp	onion powder
½ tsp	pepper
¼ tsp	salt
pinch	cayenne pepper
450 g	lean ground beef
12	mini-hamburger (slider) buns

GRILLED ONIONS

2	small cooking onions, cut crosswise in ½-inch slices
1 tsp	vegetable oil
pinch	salt

HORSERADISH SAUCE In bowl, stir together mayonnaise, mustard, horseradish and pepper. *(Make-ahead: Cover and refrigerate for up to 5 days.)*

SLIDERS In nonstick skillet, heat oil over medium-high heat; cook garlic, stirring, until fragrant, about 1 minute. Add mushrooms; cook, stirring, until golden and no liquid remains, about 8 minutes. Let cool for 5 minutes. *(Make-ahead: Let cool completely. Cover and refrigerate for up to 24 hours.)*

In bowl, stir together mushroom mixture, egg, steak sauce, mustard, onion powder, pepper, salt and cayenne pepper. Mix in beef. Shape into twelve 2½-inch wide patties. *(Make-ahead: Cover and refrigerate for up to 24 hours.)*

Place on greased grill over medium-high heat. Close lid and grill, turning once, until no longer pink inside and instant-read thermometer inserted sideways into patties reads 160°F, about 5 minutes. Transfer to plate; keep warm.

GRILLED ONIONS Meanwhile, brush both sides of onion slices with oil; sprinkle with salt. Place on greased grill; close lid and grill, turning occasionally, until golden and softened, about 8 minutes. Transfer to plate; separate into rings.

Place patties in buns; garnish with horseradish sauce and onion rings.

NUTRITIONAL INFORMATION, PER SERVING: about 173 cal, 10 g pro, 9 g total fat (3 g sat. fat), 15 g carb (1 g dietary fibre, 3 g sugar), 46 mg chol, 278 mg sodium, 236 mg potassium. % RDI: 3% calcium, 11% iron, 3% vit A, 2% vit C, 16% folate.

Grilled Rib Eye Steaks
WITH CHICKPEA MASH &
ARUGULA RADISH SALAD

HANDS-ON TIME	TOTAL TIME	MAKES
20 MINUTES	20 MINUTES	4 SERVINGS

RIB EYE STEAK Sprinkle steaks with rosemary, salt and pepper. Place on greased grill over medium-high heat; close lid and grill, turning once, until instant-read thermometer inserted in centre reads 145°F for medium-rare, about 8 minutes. Tent with foil; let stand for 4 minutes.

CHICKPEA MASH Meanwhile, in saucepan, heat oil over medium-high heat; sauté garlic until fragrant, about 1 minute. Stir in chickpeas, ⅓ cup water and the pepper; cook until warmed through, about 2 minutes. Using potato masher, coarsely mash.

ARUGULA RADISH SALAD In bowl, whisk together oil, vinegar, honey, salt and pepper; stir in arugula and radishes. Serve with steak and chickpea mash.

NUTRITIONAL INFORMATION, PER SERVING: about 545 cal, 39 g pro, 30 g total fat (8 g sat. fat), 30 g carb (6 g dietary fibre, 7 g sugar), 75 mg chol, 496 mg sodium, 683 mg potassium. % RDI: 9% calcium, 42% iron, 7% vit A, 18% vit C, 46% folate.

RIB EYE STEAKS
4	boneless rib eye grilling steaks (each about 170 g)
1 tsp	chopped fresh rosemary
¼ tsp	each salt and pepper

CHICKPEA MASH
1 tbsp	olive oil
6	cloves garlic, minced
1	can (540 mL) chickpeas, drained and rinsed
pinch	pepper

ARUGULA RADISH SALAD
3 tbsp	extra-virgin olive oil
1 tbsp	balsamic vinegar
1 tsp	liquid honey
pinch	each salt and pepper
6 cups	packed baby arugula
4	large radishes, thinly sliced

TIP FROM THE TEST KITCHEN
Letting meat stand for a few minutes after removing it from the heat helps it retain juices. Cover loosely with foil; if you cover meat tightly, it will continue cooking.

Pesto Beef Kabobs

HANDS-ON TIME	TOTAL TIME	MAKES
15 MINUTES	25 MINUTES	4 SERVINGS

500 g	top sirloin grilling steak
⅓ cup	prepared pesto
2 tbsp	olive oil
1 tbsp	wine vinegar
2	cloves garlic, minced

Cut steak into 1-inch cubes. In bowl, mix pesto, oil, vinegar and garlic; add beef and toss. Marinate for 10 minutes.

Reserving marinade, thread beef onto 8 metal or soaked wooden skewers. Place on greased grill over medium-high heat; brush with reserved marinade. Close lid and grill, turning once, until desired doneness, about 8 minutes.

NUTRITIONAL INFORMATION, PER SERVING: about 276 cal, 23 g pro, 20 g total fat (5 g sat. fat), 2 g carb (trace dietary fibre), 59 mg chol, 238 mg sodium. % RDI: 7% calcium, 20% iron, 3% vit A, 3% vit C, 5% folate.

Curried Pork Meatballs

HANDS-ON TIME	TOTAL TIME	MAKES
20 MINUTES	20 MINUTES	4 SERVINGS

450 g	lean ground pork
⅓ cup	chopped fresh cilantro
2 tbsp	mild curry paste
2 tbsp	Balkan-style plain yogurt
¼ tsp	salt

In large bowl, stir together pork, cilantro, curry paste, yogurt and salt; shape into 16 meatballs. Thread 2 meatballs onto each of 8 metal or soaked wooden skewers.

Place on greased grill over medium-high heat; close lid and grill, turning often, until no longer pink inside and instant-read thermometer inserted into meatballs reads 160°F, 10 to 12 minutes.

NUTRITIONAL INFORMATION, PER SERVING: about 237 cal, 22 g pro, 16 g total fat (5 g sat. fat), 2 g carb (1 g dietary fibre, 1 g sugar), 66 mg chol, 422 mg sodium, 327 mg potassium. % RDI: 2% calcium, 8% iron, 2% vit A, 2% vit C, 3% folate.

Peppercorn Ranch Chicken Salad

HANDS-ON TIME	TOTAL TIME	MAKES
10 MINUTES	25 MINUTES	4 SERVINGS

PEPPERCORN RANCH DRESSING In small bowl, whisk together yogurt, mayonnaise, pepper, mustard, sugar and salt. Set aside.

CHICKEN SALAD In small bowl, stir together basil, oil, mustard, salt and pepper; brush over chicken. Place on greased grill over medium heat; close lid and grill, turning once, until no longer pink inside, 12 to 15 minutes. Let cool slightly; thinly slice across the grain.

In large bowl, toss together salad greens, sprouts, cucumber and radishes, chicken strips and dressing.

NUTRITIONAL INFORMATION, PER SERVING: about 291 cal, 36 g pro, 12 g total fat (2 g sat. fat), 10 g carb (2 g dietary fibre), 87 mg chol, 435 mg sodium. % RDI: 12% calcium, 13% iron, 20% vit A, 32% vit C, 42% folate.

PEPPERCORN RANCH DRESSING

½ cup	plain yogurt
⅓ cup	light mayonnaise
1 tsp	coarsely ground pepper
½ tsp	Dijon mustard
¼ tsp	granulated sugar
pinch	salt

CHICKEN SALAD

1 tbsp	chopped fresh basil
2 tsp	vegetable oil
2 tsp	Dijon mustard
¼ tsp	each salt and pepper
2	boneless skinless chicken breasts (about 450 g total)
6 cups	torn mixed salad greens
1 cup	alfalfa sprouts
1	piece (6 inches) cucumber, sliced
½ cup	thinly sliced radishes

Grilled Caesar Salad

HANDS-ON TIME	TOTAL TIME	MAKES
20 MINUTES	40 MINUTES	4 SERVINGS

3	cloves garlic
2 tbsp	lemon juice
2 tsp	red wine vinegar
2 tsp	Worcestershire sauce
2 tsp	Dijon mustard
2	anchovy fillets, minced (or 1 tsp anchovy paste)
¼ tsp	pepper
¼ cup	extra-virgin olive oil
300 g	boneless skinless chicken breasts (about 2)
2 tbsp	light mayonnaise
4	eggs
1	demi-baguette, thinly sliced diagonally
2	hearts romaine lettuce, halved
½ cup	shaved Parmesan cheese

Mince 2 of the garlic cloves. In small bowl, whisk together minced garlic, lemon juice, vinegar, Worcestershire sauce, mustard, anchovies and pepper; drizzle in oil, whisking constantly until combined.

Transfer 2 tbsp of the dressing to separate bowl; add chicken and toss to coat. Let stand for 10 minutes.

Whisk mayonnaise into remaining dressing; set aside.

Meanwhile, in small saucepan, add eggs and enough water to cover by at least 1 inch. Cover and bring to boil over high heat; boil for 4 minutes. Drain and rinse under cold water; drain again. Peel eggs and cut in half lengthwise. Divide among 4 plates.

Place chicken on greased grill over medium-high heat; close lid and grill, turning once, until no longer pink inside, 12 to 15 minutes. Let stand for 5 minutes. Slice and divide among plates.

Place bread on grill; close lid and grill, turning once, until toasted, about 2 minutes. Halve remaining garlic clove. Rub cut sides of garlic all over bread; divide among plates.

Place romaine hearts, cut sides down, on grill over medium-high heat; close lid and grill until grill-marked and just wilting, 1 to 2 minutes. Divide among plates. Top with dressing and Parmesan.

NUTRITIONAL INFORMATION, PER SERVING: about 483 cal, 33 g pro, 27 g total fat (6 g sat. fat), 28 g carb (4 g dietary fibre, 3 g sugar), 238 mg chol, 706 mg sodium, 635 mg potassium. % RDI: 20% calcium, 26% iron, 66% vit A, 37% vit C, 75% folate.

Lemon-Basil Tilapia
WITH TOMATOES AND ZUCCHINI

HANDS-ON TIME	TOTAL TIME	MAKES
25 MINUTES	25 MINUTES	4 SERVINGS

Mix together 1 tsp of the oil, half of the basil, the lemon zest and half each of the salt and pepper; rub all over fish. Set aside.

In bowl, toss zucchini with 1 tsp of the oil and a pinch each of the salt and pepper. Place on greased grill over medium-high heat; close lid and grill, turning occasionally, until tender, about 10 minutes. Transfer to plate. Sprinkle with Parmesan; keep warm.

Meanwhile, toss together tomatoes, vinegar and remaining oil, salt and pepper. Place on greased grill; close lid and grill, turning occasionally, until softened, about 10 minutes. Transfer to plate. Sprinkle with remaining basil; keep warm.

Meanwhile, place fish on greased grill; close lid and grill, turning once, until fish flakes easily when tested, 6 to 8 minutes. Serve with zucchini and tomatoes.

NUTRITIONAL INFORMATION, PER SERVING: about 154 cal, 19 g pro, 7 g total fat (2 g sat. fat), 7 g carb (2 g dietary fibre, 6 g sugar), 36 mg chol, 376 mg sodium, 764 mg potassium. % RDI: 7% calcium, 9% iron, 22% vit A, 45% vit C, 23% folate.

1 tbsp	olive oil
1 tbsp	chopped fresh basil
½ tsp	lemon zest
½ tsp	each salt and pepper
300 g	tilapia fillets (about 2 large fillets, cut in half)
4	zucchini, cut lengthwise in quarters and seeded
2 tbsp	grated Parmesan cheese
4	plum tomatoes, halved lengthwise
2 tsp	balsamic vinegar

TIP FROM THE TEST KITCHEN
Be gentle when turning the fish; it's best to use two spatulas, placing one under and one over the fillet.

Grilled Salmon Fillets

HANDS-ON TIME	TOTAL TIME	MAKES
15 MINUTES	45 MINUTES	4 SERVINGS

⅓ **cup**	olive oil
1 tsp	grated lemon zest
¼ cup	lemon juice
2 tbsp	chopped fresh dill
¼ tsp	each salt and pepper
4	skin-on salmon fillets (about 500 g total)

Whisk together oil, lemon zest, lemon juice, dill, salt and pepper; pour into shallow dish. Add salmon, turning to coat. Cover and refrigerate, turning occasionally, for up to 30 minutes.

Remove salmon from marinade, reserving excess. Place salmon, skin side down, on greased grill over medium-high heat; close lid and grill, basting frequently with reserved marinade, until fish flakes easily when tested, about 10 minutes.

NUTRITIONAL INFORMATION, PER SERVING: about 341 cal, 19 g pro, 29 g total fat (5 g sat. fat), 2 g carb (trace dietary fibre, trace sugar), 54 mg chol, 197 mg sodium, 355 mg potassium. % RDI: 1% calcium, 4% iron, 2% vit A, 18% vit C, 15% folate.

TIP FROM THE TEST KITCHEN
Grilling salmon fillets with the skin on helps keep the fish moist. Once the fish is cooked, slip a spatula between the skin and fish; lift the fish, leaving the skin on the grill. Just don't forget to remove the skin and clean the grill after dinner.

Grilled Vegetables
WITH CHIMICHURRI SAUCE

HANDS-ON TIME	TOTAL TIME	MAKES
15 MINUTES	25 MINUTES	6 SERVINGS

CHIMICHURRI SAUCE In food processor, pulse together basil, parsley, mint, garlic, salt, pepper and hot pepper flakes. Add oil, vinegar and 2 tbsp of water; pulse until mixture becomes smooth paste.

GRILLED VEGETABLES Halve, seed and core peppers; cut each half into thirds. Sprinkle peppers and zucchini with salt and pepper.

Place peppers and zucchini on greased grill over medium-high heat; close lid and grill, turning once, until tender, 12 to 15 minutes. Brush vegetables with half of the chimichurri sauce; serve with remaining sauce.

NUTRITIONAL INFORMATION, PER SERVING: about 125 cal, 3 g pro, 10 g total fat (1 g sat. fat), 9 g carb (3 g dietary fibre, 6 g sugar), 0 mg chol, 106 mg sodium, 539 mg potassium. % RDI: 5% calcium, 14% iron, 29% vit A, 238% vit C, 29% folate.

CHIMICHURRI SAUCE

1 cup	packed fresh basil leaves
½ cup	fresh parsley
⅓ cup	fresh mint
1	clove garlic, minced
¼ tsp	each salt and pepper
pinch	hot pepper flakes
¼ cup	extra-virgin olive oil
1 tbsp	red wine vinegar

GRILLED VEGETABLES

2	sweet orange peppers
2	sweet yellow peppers
4	zucchini, cut lengthwise in ½-inch thick slices
pinch	each salt and pepper

TIP FROM THE TEST KITCHEN
Use leftover grilled peppers and zucchini on sandwiches, chop them into a salad or mix them into a frittata.

Curried Chicken Skewers
WITH CREAMY CHICKPEA SALAD

HANDS-ON TIME 15 MINUTES	TOTAL TIME 15 MINUTES	MAKES 4 SERVINGS

CURRIED CHICKEN

2 tbsp	plain Balkan-style yogurt
1 tbsp	mild curry paste
2	cloves garlic, pressed or grated
pinch	salt
450 g	boneless skinless chicken breasts, cut in 24 cubes

CHICKPEA SALAD

¼ cup	plain Balkan-style yogurt
¼ cup	light mayonnaise
1½ tsp	grated fresh ginger
1	small clove garlic, pressed or grated
pinch	each salt and pepper
1	can (540 mL) chickpeas, drained, rinsed and patted dry
1 cup	finely chopped cucumber
¼ cup	chopped fresh cilantro
2	green onions, sliced
1	rib celery, diced

CURRIED CHICKEN In bowl, stir together yogurt, curry paste, garlic and salt; add chicken and stir to coat. Thread 3 pieces of the chicken onto each of 8 metal or soaked wooden skewers. Place on greased grill over medium-high heat; close lid and grill, turning once, until no longer pink inside, about 8 minutes.

CHICKPEA SALAD Meanwhile, in large bowl, whisk together yogurt, mayonnaise, ginger, garlic, salt and pepper. Add chickpeas, cucumber, cilantro, green onions and celery; stir to coat. Serve with chicken.

NUTRITIONAL INFORMATION, PER SERVING: about 331 cal, 33 g pro, 12 g total fat (2 g sat. fat), 24 g carb (6 g dietary fibre, 5 g sugar), 75 mg chol, 449 mg sodium, 555 mg potassium. % RDI: 8% calcium, 11% iron, 5% vit A, 7% vit C, 21% folate.

TIP FROM THE TEST KITCHEN
You can toss the chicken with the yogurt-curry mixture up to 24 hours ahead; store in an airtight container in the fridge.

INDEX

CONTRIBUTORS

RECIPES
All recipes were developed and Tested Till Perfect by the Canadian Living Test Kitchen

PHOTOGRAPHY
JESSE BRIOUX 31
RYAN BROOK 26
JEFF COULSON back cover (left, third from top; centre); 4, 5 (top), 13, 14, 18, 32, 37, 38, 67, 74, 80, 87, 88, 93, 94, 97, 103, 104, 110, 113, 128, 133, 139, 140, 145, 146, 151
ANGUS FERGUSSON back cover (left, top; right); 43, 49, 50, 53, 121, 127
STEVE KRUG 7, 25
JODI PUDGE front cover; 8, 61, 62, 68, 79, 109, 114
ROBERT TSANG 5 (bottom)
JAMES TSE 44
MAYA VISNYEI back cover (left, second from top; left, bottom); p.17, 54, 73, 98, 122, 134

FOOD STYLING
BERNADETTE AMMAR 4
ASHLEY DENTON 44, 109
MICHAEL ELLIOTT front cover; back cover (left, top; right); 5 (bottom) 8, 43, 49, 50, 53, 54, 61, 68, 98, 127
HEATHER ELOPH 14, 113
DAVID GRENIER back cover (left, third from top; centre); 5 (top), 13, 18, 32, 38, 62, 67, 74, 79, 87, 88, 94, 97, 110, 128, 133, 139, 140, 146, 151
ADELE HAGAN 145
ESHUN MOTT 31
CHRISTOPHER ST. ONGE 37, 121
CLAIRE STUBBS back cover (left, second from top; left, bottom); 17, 73, 103, 114, 122, 134
MELANIE STUPARYK 26, 80, 93
NOAH WHITENOFF 7, 25, 104

PROP STYLING
LAURA BRANSON 5 (bottom), 26, 145
AURALIE BRYCE 14, 104, 113, 146
CATHERINE DOHERTY front cover; back cover (centre); 8, 13, 18, 38, 44, 61, 67, 68, 88, 103, 114, 121
JENNIFER EVANS 7, 25, 54, 62, 79, 98, 109
MADELEINE JOHARI back cover (left, top; centre); 43, 49, 50, 53, 80, 92, 127
SABRINA LINN 32, 74, 87, 94, 110, 139
SASHA SEYMOUR 4, 31, 37, 128, 133, 140
CAROLYN SOUCH back cover (left, third from top); 5 (top), 97, 151
PAGE WEIR back cover (left, second from top; left, bottom); 17, 73, 122, 134

About Our Nutrition Information

To meet nutrient needs each day, moderately active women aged 25 to 49 need about 1,900 calories, 51 g protein, 261 g carbohydrate, 25 to 35 g fibre and not more than 63 g total fat (21 g saturated fat). Men and teenagers usually need more. Canadian sodium intake of approximately 3,500 mg daily should be reduced, whereas the intake of potassium from food sources should be increased to 4,700 mg per day. The percentage of recommended daily intake (% RDI) is based on the values used for Canadian food labels for calcium, iron, vitamins A and C, and folate.

Figures are rounded off. They are based on the first ingredient listed when there is a choice and do not include optional ingredients or those with no specified amounts.

ABBREVIATIONS

cal = calories
pro = protein
carb = carbohydrate
sat. fat = saturated fat
chol = cholesterol

ZUCCHINI RIBBON
AND CAPER PASTA
p.137

Canadian Living

Complete your collection of Tested-Till-Perfect recipes!

canadianliving.com/books